Forex Trading
beginners 2021

Strategies, Secrets and How to Manage the Risk and Your Money

Kenny Evans

Table of Contents

INTRODUCTION

So what is Forex? Have you heard of it? A quick search online will most likely give you the following definitions: "Foreign Exchange", "any type of financial instrument that is used to make payments between countries", "refers to off-exchange foreign currency transactions. The term can also refer to some on-exchange transactions as well", "simultaneously buying one currency and selling another", "(forex, FX, or currency market) is a worldwide decentralized over-the-counter financial market for the trading of currencies", and "the market where one currency is traded for another. It is one of the largest markets in the world".

Those definitions can be pretty self-explanatory but in a nutshell, Forex or Forex trading is the buying and selling of currencies and you can make money from that if you know how to get it done right. If you happen to be planning to venture into Internet marketing or try online jobs as either alternative or extra source of income, you might want to try Forex trading. In fact, a lot of people in the whole world are eyeing this type of online career.

Why they do that and why you should try it as well is explained in the following paragraphs.

Now that the question - what is Forex? - has been answered and clear to you, the next thing you, as a newbie, need to learn is how it works. If you do study the whole Forex trading process, you will understand why so many individuals would like to take a shot with this job. One known reason is that doing Forex trading is quite convenient compared to other online jobs (you don't have to write, you don't have to advertise, you don't have to create a website, etc.) and offline work (you don't have to take orders, you don't have to clean glass windows, you don't have to check electrical wires, etc.) as well. Most

Forex trading systems can be run with little or no supervision at all because of those automated software and Forex robots. You can now spend some more time with your family if that's what you want.

Although Forex trading can be convenient, that doesn't necessarily mean it's that easy. Some traders find it great to have a convenient yet challenging task. Sure, it's automated and all that but a wise Forex trader or Internet marketer knows that in order to make the most out of this Forex trading system, one should not just rely entirely on automated software, signal providers, expert advisors, Forex robots and the like. Don't let them do the whole job for you because you know for a fact that you can do better than those so-called tools combined. Don't be a lazy ass.

Perhaps one of the biggest, if not the biggest, reasons behind the huge following of the Forex market is the fact that it is such a lucrative opportunity online. If you know what you are doing and you are doing it right, you can earn profits tenfold than your previous job or what you can ever imagine. Here, you can work as much and you can earn as much too. The question now is: what is Forex to you? If you think it's the job you want to pursue then by all means, go for it.

How do people get rich? Other than making savings in every month of doing hard work and determination, people get there by doing investments. The really rich people get involve in the foreign exchange market or better known as the Forex.

So what is Forex Trading and how does it help you earn fast money? Forex is basically about making trading of buying and selling of the currencies in the world. A currency of a country has difference in values than another country's currency and also a value of money today is different than the value of money tomorrow. Therefore, it is from this money value that we can do buying and selling and later earn profits.

In the Forex trading, there are the highest trading currencies which come in four pairs. They are the major business traders in the world, namely the Euro with US Dollar, the US Dollar with Japanese Yen, the US Dollar with Swiss Franc and the US Dollar with British Pound. It has an amount of over $1.9 trillion being traded daily, making the Forex Trading as the largest financial market in the globe. However global this money trading is the Forex trading works without having a physical location and not even there is a central exchange. It runs within a huge network of banks all over the world, corporations and individuals who does trading of a currency for another. Whatever the time is, there will have trading going on in different parts of the world. Thus, unlike the domestic stock markets that only operates on working hours, Forex currency trading operates in a 24 hours a day basis. As long as every country involves in the forex market trading, the market will open all day.

In the earlier times before Forex is introduced and widely used by many, currency trading is difficult to enter because of high barriers. The foreign exchange market could only be accessed by the retail investors through banks that do large amounts of currency transactions for the purpose of commercials or investments. That makes only the large banking organizations and institutional firms that could trade in forex. Then, in 1971, the exchange rates were let to float freely and have made the trading volume increased tremendously. Up until today, the forex market is used by importers and exporters, multinational corporations, speculators, international portfolio managers, long-term holders, and day traders to do their payments for all kinds of goods and services that make businesses running. They also make transactions in financial assets.

It is well-known by Forex traders that the rule of earning money through Forex is by buying low and selling high. However, there is a trick on earning smart money by knowing the right time to buy and to sell. It is a matter of speculation. Graphs are often used to help traders make decisions. Business trends and strategies are also being released in the news every day. But making decisions for the next step is always by predictions based on the previous performance and activity. The politics of a country and how it is running can also be a good measuring aid for analyzing the currency value patterns. Therefore, to be an active trader with smart guesses, one must be aware of the current issues in the national news of the country.

It sure is exciting if you are able to earn a huge amount of money over Forex. But still, the system can be very complex and it may also be risky. It is recommended that a beginner in Forex reads a lot and finds information before opening an account for Forex.

Just what is Forex, Fx, Foreign Exchange? Only the largest financial enterprise on the planet! With more than $2 trillion changing hands everyday the Foreign Exchange market, Forex or FX market, are all the terms that are used to describe the business of the trading of the worlds various currencies. Engaging in hundreds of times the daily trading that happens on the New York Stock Exchange and having its beginning in 1971 the Foreign Exchange Market is where money is sold and bought freely. Forex has become the largest liquid financial market today. Forex is also a non-stop cash market where you speculate on changes in exchange rates of foreign currencies. Forex operates through a global network of banks, corporations and individuals trading one currency for another but have no physical location and no central exchange unlike other financial markets.

FOREX is a perfect market to invest in, as it is free from any external control and free competition. The Foreign Exchange market place is distinguished from the others because of its high trading volume and geographical dispersion. A trader with sound knowledge of currency trading can earn a substantial profit in the forex market. Along with the knowledge of trading, he or she should have access to a few tools of forex trading. These tools are made to strengthen the confidence of a trader and can prove out to be a great help for a winning currency trading in forex.

A Good Forex trader should also know that trying to trade in the Forex market without a broker could lead to damaging results for the normal trader. Determining a Forex broker is a tough process to maneuver through and for most people, the need for external assistance is vital and necessary. Indeed, it is very important that you do your due diligence when researching any future brokerage firms to handle your financial portfolio. A serious Forex Broker will provide a potential customer with clients that are successful because of using their firm and can attest to the specific broker's qualifications and achiever records. One other factor in determining a sincere Forex broker is the margin of return that is offered. A Forex trading margin used to influence your money and many Forex brokers offer different margins. Determining a Forex broker, who gives a margin of ten to one isn't a very good find so it's worth the time to invest in more research.

In years past, just some banks and large lending and financial institutions were the only entities allowed to utilize the Forex market. That is no longer the case, largely because of the technological advancements and the ability by way of the internet, individuals, government agencies and even brokerage firms now have the ability also to do forex trading on the Internet. With a computer, a keyboard and mouse, you too can now become a forex trader. In other words it does not require A financial degree to be able to trade forex. Learning how is very easy and you will need to learn how, in order to become a successful investor on the Foreign Exchange Market.

Above all you need not be troubled or afraid, this same internet has plenty of websites that can and will give you the opportunity to "Paper Trade" before you ever think of going live.

Forex trading is now quite an acceptable occupation for private individuals. It used to be only available to top financial institutions, but the internet has enabled everyone, even people with a low starting capital, to trade the forex markets. So what makes forex trading so attractive?

Well the most obvious attraction is the earning potential. The amount of money you can make from forex trading is unlimited. The sky really is the limit. If you have a consistently profitable strategy, then you can use leverage to multiply your earnings. For example, if a forex broker offers 1:100 leverage, this means you can trade a $100,000 position with just $1000 and a $10,000 position with just $100.

This means that if you are successful your earnings will grow rapidly. Compare this with traditional share trading where if you wanted to buy $100,000 worth of shares, then you would have to have $100,000 in capital.

Another huge draw is the fact that the forex markets are open 24 hours a day during the week. So you can therefore trade during the hours that suit you. Plus there's the fact that liquidity is always high as currencies are traded in countries all around the world, which means that you will generally not have any trouble getting a large position filled at any time of the day.

Another advantage of forex trading is that it is very easy to open an account with a broker and start trading shortly afterwards. There are many top forex brokers nowadays and a lot of them have excellent trading platforms as well as top of the range charting software that you can use to make your trading decisions.

Charts are one of the key tools for any trader as they are invaluable in helping you to find possible trades. They are useful when trading any financial instrument, but they are particularly useful when trading forex because the price, particularly of the major currency pairs, generally conforms extremely well to technical analysis.

So overall there any many reasons why forex trading is becoming so popular. Of course it's very easy to start trading forex, but it's a lot harder to actually make money consistently from forex trading. This is why I recommend starting off by using a free demo account as this will enable you to become familiar with trading, without risking any of your own money. There is a steep learning curve and it's always best to come up with some form of trading system before trading for real.

CHAPTER 1

WHAT IS FOREX?

Most professionals may not be able to answer the question truthfully. So what is forex then? Forex, the simple term for foreign exchange, is among the most important element of a country's economy. Forex market refers to the trading of one currency for another. This is considered as the most liquid financial market that is participated by banks, multinational corporations, currency speculators, governements, and other financial markets and institutions.

Basically, there are four currency pairs dominating the percentage rates in the forex market. These include the British Pound and USD; Japanese Yen and USD; USD and Euro Dollar; and Swiss Franc and USD. These monetary tools hold a currency that should appreciate in value, relative to other currencies.

The process of trading in forex is normally held 24 hours a day around the globe. Meaning, when the Asian trading closes, the European and American transactions start. Forex traders participate in the process using their forex software, which keep them on track with the past, present, and future trading details. The use of such software is not that easy that's why many forex professionals undergo extensive training before practicing the high-profitable career. Nonetheless, some forex software are made user-friendly, from which you can find multilingual currency converter for over 160 currencies.

The basics in forex marketing can be learned online or in school. The use of tools and systems would be among the basics. Hence, there are a lot to know more. Among the most important ones are the ones affecting the economy, politics, and market psychology. Warning about cases of forex scams should also be emphasized.

WHAT IS FOREX?

Forex or FX market is the international Foreign Exchange market. Forex trading turns over approximately 1.5 trillion to 3 trillion US dollars daily! Hundreds of thousands of people participate in Forex trading as a means to make money. Forex trading is a very lucrative method of making BIG money over a short period of time. Like every business venture Forex trading involves risks, my best advice to you is start small and grow big! Never invest more money than you can afford to lose!

Forex trading refers to foreign exchange trading - the trading of currencies from various countries. People who trade forex will exchange one currency for another in the hopes that the currency that they bought goes up in value in comparison to the one they exchanged it for.

As an example, if I think the EURO is going to go up versus the US dollar, then I can buy EURO by exchanging US dollars. If I'm right and the EURO goes up in value, then I make a profit.

People who trade currencies will use various techniques to try to determine which currencies are going to go up and which are going to go down. There are certainly many different strategies available, but if you're a beginner wondering what is forex trading you can actually use a forex trading program that will point out trading opportunities for you.

These programs are also called "forex robots" and anaylze the markets by looking at price history, movements and other indicators. They then look for patterns and indicators that have the potential to signal a winning trade.

Anyone, beginners included, can use a forex robot. The nice thing about these programs is that they have been programmed by trading professionals that have years of experience in the markets. The trading decisions are made from these years of expertise.

By using a program like this, you have the chance to make some great profits whether you're a beginner or a veteran. It's impressive how well many of these work.

Forex trading involves a trader buying and selling different currency pairs. Such pairs include the EUR/USD or the Euro Dollar and the US Dollar and the GBP/JPY or the British Pound and the Japanese Yen. There are a wide variety of different currency pairs or crosses that you can trade. Similar to investing in stocks, Forex trading involves either buying or selling a currency pair with the belief that it will either go up or down and you will profit based on the price you purchased at and by how far it moves.

Why would anyone want to trade the Forex markets over the more traditional stock market? The main reason is that for 5 days a week the Forex market is a 24 hour market. Unlike the stock market, you can open and close your trades in Forex anytime of the day. The market is almost never closed (except on weekends), this allows you to buy and sell whenever you like. The second main reason is because many currency pairs in the Forex market are volatile. This volatility promises large profits if a trader is fortunate enough to be on the right side of the trade.

Forex trading is similar to most other more traditional styles of trading. However, instead of purchasing stocks or bonds, you buy and sell currency pairs with the belief that you will profit from its movement.
With online forex trading becoming a more and more popular and lucrative option to make money online as
well as offline, it is hardly surprising that there is an increase of novice traders in the field. However, before you actually start investing money into currency trading, it is important to understand what is forex as well as have an insight into the market and its ways.

What is forex can simply be answered by the fact that it deals with the exchange of foreign currencies in pairs. In other words, it is defined as the buying and selling of currency, where one person buys another currency using a different currency. Commonly traded currencies are the US Dollar, British Pounds, Japanese Yen and the Euro.

It is important to understand that each currency has its own value against the other in the global market, which is called the exchange rate. In other words, currencies are traded in pairs, where the first currency is the base currency and the second is the quote currency. The base currency is always valued at 1 and is the numerator while the quote currency is the denominator and changes according to the fluctuations in the market. For example, in the currency pair GBP/JPY, British Pounds or GBP is the base currency and JPY or Japanese Yen is the quote currency. Where GBP/JPY is 150, it means that in order to get 1 British Pound you have to pay 150 Japanese Yen.

It is interesting to note that in the initial days of forex trading, only banks, institutions and groups were allowed to trade in foreign currencies, making it an exclusive trade. However, with the passage of time, more and more individual traders started entering the market, which effectively put an end to the exclusive nature of this market. Today, with the help of a PC, internet connection and little money, you can start trading in the foreign exchange market without any hassle.

It is necessary to add here that while entering the forex market is easy, sustaining your investment and making a profit requires skill, knowledge and determination, which can be easily learned from various sources. Given the popularity of online forex trading, there are several schools and workshops, both online as well as offline, which deal with the basics of forex trading, right from the basic questions of what is forex to the ways and means that you can adopt for continuous profits.

SO WHAT IS 'FOREX'?

The word 'Forex' is simply a shortening of 'Foreign Exchange'. Forex trading is when traders buy and sell different currencies from one currency to another.

So, for example, if you were to buy the European currency (the Euro, EUR) with US Dollars (symbol USD), then you would be 'buying the Euro' and at the same time 'selling the US Dollar'. You would effectively be betting that the value of the Euro compared to the

Dollar would increase to have any chance of receiving a profit. Another way of thinking about this trade is that you are going 'Long' on the EUR/USD.

Many people find this concept a little tricky to understand. Why would this particular trade be selling the Dollar? Well, if the Dollar were to drop in value compared to the Euro (remember that you have bought your Euros with US Dollars), then you would be able to buy back more Dollars than you started with, using the Euros which have become more valuable in relative terms. In other words, you would have profited from the decline of the Dollar.

Base and Quote Currencies the first currency quoted in a currency pair is called the base currency and the second currency is called the quote currency. In the above example, the base currency is the Euro and the quote currency is the US Dollar.
So you may see a quote like this:

EUR/USD = 1.2288

This means that 1 Euro (the base currency) is presently worth 1.2288 US Dollars (the quote currency).

Forex traders usually place a trade through a broker who have direct access to the fx market via an associated partner in the Interbank Market. When you close out your trade, your broker will close the position with this partner and calculate the loss or gain on the trade, which is then applied to your brokerage account. These days,

high speed communications and technologies which link all players in the FX market mean that trades can be opened and closed in a matter of seconds.

FOREX TRADE EXAMPLE

Here's an example of a currency trade. Suppose you thought that the Euro was going to weaken compared to the US dollar in the coming weeks (note that forex traders can trade on timescales ranging from minutes to years). This time, going short on the EUR/USD assuming this belief turns out to be correct would be a smart move.

There are no 'shorting' restrictions in the forex market (unlike the stock market) so this trade would be very
straight forward to place through your broker as long as you had the required deposit.

So the quote today might be:
EUR/USD = 1.2288

You think the Euro will decline in value against the USD, so you place a short order on this currency pair and purchase 1000 Euros. This costs you $1228.80 US Dollars.

The next week, the quote is now:
EUR/USD = 1.2008

1 Euro is now only worth $1.2008 US Dollars. Having shorted this currency pair (which is the same as going long on the USD/EUR opposite currency pair), you will have made a profit of $0.0280 x 1000 = $28.

Note, it is important to realize that your broker will take a brokerage fee from both placing the trade and closing out the trade, whether or not you make a profit. Forex currency pairs are usually traded on futures markets such as the Chicago Mercantile Exchange (CME).

WANT TO LEARN MORE ABOUT HOW TO START AS A FOREX TRADER? DON'T KNOW WHERE TO START?

A strong understanding of the basic principles for success in FX trading is ESSENTIAL, or you risk losing your trading capital FAST (like some people who think they don't need Forex trading training).

The forex market is one of largest financial markets in the world. And the amazing thing is that Sunday to Friday, it is a 24 hour market, it does not close daily like the stock market. Further, it is an international market, so it is bigger than almost any domestic stock market could ever be. Speculators on the forex market make money depending on the movements of the market and many have their own forex trading strategy. The most widely traded currencies are the US Dollar, the Euro, the British Pound, and the Japanese Yen. As you can see, these are the world's most powerful economies, implying that due to the amount of trade going on in these countries, businesses in these countries need plenty of foreign exchange.

As a speculator or forex trader, one would take a position on a country, depending on what one believes are the future prospects for that country and then either buy or sell its currency. For instance, if you believe that the US dollar will depreciate against the Euro, as a forex trader, you would sell US dollars right now at a higher price with the expectation of buying them from the market at a lower price when the US dollar depreciates. You will make the differential between the higher price and the lower price per dollar that you sold.

Since you did not actually have stock of US dollars at the time you sold, this is called a short position.

The opposite of this is a long position, meaning that you believe the US dollar will appreciate and as a forex trader, you buy US dollars in hopes of selling them at a higher price when the market for them goes up. This is a simple long trade. There are plenty of forex currency trading systems to help you maximize your profitability.

An understanding of factors that go into successful forex currency trading is essential when you decide to become a forex trader, or maybe eventually a broker. The main factors that interact to form the time, currency, interest rates and understanding of these elements what makes a good forex trader.

basis for the trade are exchange rates. A solid and their interplay is the internet is a big driving force in the increased popularity of forex currency trading. With the introduction of the internet into every home, the average person now has gained access to the huge forex market. Earlier a playground for rich individual investors or huge institutions like financial companies and banks, the international forex market is now open to you and millions of others. And people are already tapping it to make their private fortunes.

WHAT IS FOREX DEMO ACCOUNT? UNDERSTANDING HOW FOREX PRACTICE ACCOUNT WORKS

The forex market is becoming more and more popular. This is because it is one of the fastest ways to get rich (also the fastest way to get broke if you are not careful). The internet has made Forex trading far more popular than it used to be in the past when trading was limited only to big corporations and banks.

The popularity of the Forex trading market also means there are many who have little or no experience but want to leverage of the power of the Forex market to make some money. This is why almost all Forex coach will advise new Forex traders to start trading with a Forex demo account or Forex practice account.

What Is Forex Demo Account?

A Forex demo account or Forex practice account is a Forex trading accounts that allows you to trade with "unreal" money. This type of account allows you to test your trading skills or strategies without any risk whatsoever. After you have read so many Forex trading books, attended seminars and workshops, it is better applying what you have learnt using a Forex practice account. It lets you feel how it is like trading with real money in the Forex market but this time with risk. Trading with a demo account is the bes way to get started as a new trader but don't get stuck in it. No matter how hard you try, you cannot move up to the next level of trading until you learn how to risk real money. That is exactly what the Forex market is all about. The key to succeeding as a Forex trader is to open a live account after a period of demo trading and start out slowly.

WHAT IS A FOREX ROBOT?

If you could hire the best Stock Broker to work for you 24 hours a day, 7 days a week, and give you the best trading advice for only a few hundred dollars per year, would you be interested? My guess is YES! Well, in simple terms, a Forex robot also known as a Forex Trading Robot is similar to a virtual stock broker. A Forex robot will give you

Forex trading advice 24/7, this sophisticated trading software will advice you about what foreign currency to buy or sell. It is constantly monitoring international markets even whilst you are sleeping! Forex robots are ideal for busy people who are always on the go, they are also and deal for newbie's, people who are new to the forex market with little skill or experience.

To use a Forex Robot (forex system) first you must have a computer and internet access. You simply sign-up online with a company that offers a Forex Robot, pay a small membership fee, then you can login 24/7 to get predictions and trade online.

CHAPTER 2

ADVANTAGES OF TRADING FOREX

There are many advantages to Trading FOREX as your main income generator. Let's start by something that may be worrying you already. "Do I need a Diploma or some kind of Certification to trade FOREX?" The answer is this:

When attempting to make more profit than losses on the fluctuation of exchange rates between major currencies (i.e., Trading the FOREX), nobody is going to ask you for a diploma, a formal license or verify the amount of hours you've spent studying the Foreign exchange market and banking industry. All you need is the proper training.

But this is not the only advantage you get when trading FOREX compared to other ways of investment and speculation; i.e. Stocks and Commodities. You have a whole bunch of advantages over these other ptions that will be enumerated in the following paragraphs.

Fifteen years ago when the economic gloom descended on the world, most conservative investments no longer held any attraction for the average middle class investor. Such was the need of instant liquidity that the usual bank securities, mutual funds and stocks quickly faded into the background. Yet, gaining in stature and solidity was Foreign Exchange (Forex) trading. This, however, was to remain the exclusive domain of the big time investor for some length of time.

Not surprisingly, when the doors were wide open to the public at last, there were very few smiles. The majority of the new traders, without any experience or trading skills, were quick to part with their money in undue haste. And, while they only had themselves to blame, they were less than charitable. There was "no money to be made" they chanted and declared forex a scam. Little did they realize that if that was so, trading in foreign exchange would not have hit a staggering high of $4.9 trillion in daily trades as it stands today. This makes it at least 30 times bigger than the Nasdaq and the NYSE.

At the beginning it must be understood that foreign currencies is what all nations need to buy goods from one another. Similarly, if you choose to visit a foreign country, you will be required to make all payments in the currency of that country. The prices of these currencies are prone to fluctuation from time to time depending on economic, political and reasons attributable to nature. Another reason is supply and demand. For example when there is a greater need of the U.S. Dollar, the cost of the dollar will rise. Conversely, when this currency is in excess, the price is liable to go down. Yet, the more prominent currencies like the U.S. Dollar, the British Pound Sterling, the Euro and the Japanese Yen are less prone to fluctuations in comparison to other currencies.

The foreign exchange market determines the relative values of different currencies. It is the largest market in the world and yet there is no central marketplace for the exchange of currency. Instead all business is conducted over-the-counter and online. This decentralization offers traders the opportunity to choose from different traders to make trades with, at competitive prices.

Whereas, in the stock market the trading is in commodities that bring in the profits, forex trading deals only in currencies where the choice of currency of one country is pitted against the other. This market is open twenty-four hours a day, five days a week, with currencies being traded around the world in all of the major financial centers.

As it stands, the forex business appears remarkably simple for beginners to comprehend. What needs knowledge and experience is the expertise to open a trading position at the opportune moment and close it with profit. That is all there is to it. But in the hard world of financial reality, successful trading is carried out in a professional, systematic and scientific way. The ultimate aim is that small but consistent gains generate positive results and capital growth over the long-term.

To ensure handsome profits from currency trading, it is recommended that you gain some knowledge about the Foreign Exchange market first and then practice in a demo account with one of the brokers. Save yourself the unfortunate experience of rushing in, trading with real money and emerging desolate and empty handed.

"It's best to delve into different asset classes," says a financial expert: "Most of the general public is used to trading in equities. It's best to diversify, and the forex market is many times bigger, and more liquid."

THE MAIN BENEFITS OF TRADING THE FX SPOT MARKET:

1): FOREX is the largest financial market in the world.

With a daily trading volume of over $1.5 trillion, the spot FOREX market can absorb trading sizes that dwarf the capacity of any other market. In fact, when compared with the $50 billion daily market for equities or the $30 billion futures market, it becomes quickly apparent this gives you, and millions of other FOREX traders, almost infinite trading liquidity and flexibility.

2): FOREX is a TRUE 24-hour market.

The FOREX Market never sleeps. Trading positions can be entered and exited at any moment - around the globe, around the clock, six days a week. There is no waiting for an opening bell as in the case of trading stocks. It is a 24-hour, continuous electronic (ONLINE) currency exchange that never closes. This is very desirable for you if you want to trade on a part-time basis, because you can choose when you want to trade: morning, noon or night.
3): There is never a Bear Market in FOREX.

You can have access to a seamless, mutually-inclusive (two- way) exchange of currencies. Meaning, because currencies trade in "pairs" (for example, US dollar vs. yen or US dollar vs. Swiss franc), one side of every currency pair (for example, USD/JPY - JPY = YEN) is constantly moving in relation to the other. Thus, when you buy a particular currency, you are actually simultaneously selling the other currency in that particular pair. As the market moves, one of the currencies will increase in value versus the other. Of course, it is up to you to choose the correct currency to be long or short. Since currency trading always involves buying one currency and selling another, there is no structural bias to the market. This means you have equal potential to profit in both a rising or falling market.

4): High Leverage - up to 200:1 Leverage.

You are permitted to trade foreign currencies on a highly leveraged basis - up to 200 times your investment with some brokers. This is primarily attributed to the higher levels of liquidity within the currency markets. Standard 100,000- unit currency lots can be traded with as little as 1% margin, or $1,000. Mini FX accounts are permitted to trade with just 0.5% margin -- in other words, just $50 allows you to control a 10,000-unit currency position. Futures traders, who are accustomed to margin requirements generally equal to 5%-8% of the contract value, will immediately recognize that the FOREX market provides much greater leverage, and for stock traders, who must post at least 50% margin, thereâ€™s no comparison. If you are looking for an efficient use of trading capital, this is it!

5): Price Movements Are Highly Predictable.

Although currency prices in the FX market may be volatile, they generally repeat themselves in relatively predictable cycles, creating trends. The strong trends that foreign currencies develop are a significant advantage for traders who use the correct "technical" methods.
Unlike stocks, currencies rarely spend much time in tight trading ranges and have the tendency to develop strong trends. Over 80% of volume is speculative in nature and, as a result, the market frequently overshoots and then corrects itself. As a technically-trained trader, you can easily identify new trends and breakouts, which provide for multiple opportunities to enter and exit positions.

6:) Commission-free Trading and Low Transaction Cost

When you trade FOREX, through one of our recommended brokers(this info is in our private resources section), you'll do it totally commission-free! These brokers don't charge commissions to trade or to maintain an account, and that goes for all clients trading the FOREX through them, regardless of your account balance or trading volume. Even Mini FX traders can buy and sell currencies online, commission-free.

What about trading fees? There are none of the usual fees to which futures and equity traders are accustomed - no exchange or clearing fees, no N_F_A or S_E_C fees. Because currencies trade over-the-counter (OTC), via a global electronic network -- in FOREX, what you see is what you get, allowing you to make quick decisions on your trades without having to worry or account for fees that may affect your profit/loss or slippage.

In the equities markets, you must pay both a commission and exchange fees. The over-the-counter structure of the FX market eliminates exchange and clearing fees, which in turn lowers transaction costs.

So, if FOREX broker don't charge commissions, how do they make money? Like all traded financial products, over-the- counter currency trading involves a bid/ask spread, which represents the prices at which your counterparty is willing to trade. Because the currency market offers round-the-clock liquidity, you receive tight, competitive spreads both intra-day and night. Stock traders can be more vulnerable to liquidity risk and typically receive wider trading spreads, especially during after-hours trading.

7): Instantaneous Order Execution and Market Transparency.

Market transparency is highly desired in any trading environment. The greater the market transparency, the more efficient the market becomes. Unlike other markets where transparency is compromised (like in the Enron scandal), FOREX markets are highly transparent (i.e., analyzing countries, and having access to real-time research / news, is easier than companies).

Because of this transparency, as an FX trader, you will be able to exercise risk management strategies in accordance to the fundamental and technical indicators we teach at RapidForex.com

The FX market offers the highest level of market transparency out of all the financial markets. Because of this, order execution and fill confirmation usually occur in just 1-2 seconds. Markets that do not offer executable prices and force traders to absorb slippage obviously compromise the trader's profit potential considerably.

In the forex world, order execution is all-electronic and because you'll be trading via an Internet-based platform, instantaneous execution is routine. There are no exchanges, no traditional open-outcry pits, no floor brokers, and consequently, no delays.

Forex trading is typically done through a broker, also referred to as a market maker. The leading ones offer email alerts, incomparable forex signals service with a sophisticated trade copier. Once you have set up your account with one of them, you will seldom be required to do another thing. Monthly memberships are designed to suit your convenience and come at a nominal price.

The good news is that U.S. based forex brokers have reported an average of 28.5% profitability, with some brokers claiming profitability results as high as 50%. Hopefully, these are facts that should resolve any doubts one may harbor about the possibility of making money in forex trading.

Finally, if investing in forex has got you interested, why not give it a try for a few months. Who knows what begins as a trial venture may end up becoming a satisfying addiction for life?

CHAPTER 3

WHEN THE FOREX MARKET IS OPEN

There is a common misconception that the Forex market is open 24 hours a day seven days a week. Theoretically the global Forex market is open 24 hours seven days a week but an individual is still limited to the hours he can trade. Opposed to other regulated markets such as that of the stock exchange the Forex market is a network of financial institutions and retail trading brokers which gives them the ability to create their own hours of operation. Forex hours of operation are in accordance to their time zone. Most establishments trade between the hours of 8 a.m. to 4 p.m. relative to their local time zone.

On average the Forex market is available for trading 24 hours a day along with 5 1/2 days per week. It should also be noted that most veteran day traders understand that there are more profitable trades conducted when market activity is high during working hours. In other words it is possible to trade at any time of the day, late at night even, but it might not necessarily be the most profitable time due to light activity.

Many experts suggest that you should concentrate your trading hours in accordance to the three largest Forex currency market centers which include London, New York, and Tokyo. By targeting these three major markets you can fully utilize the maximum market activity and have the greatest potential for being successful in your daily Forex trading. Market specialist also suggest that the most serious Forex traders specifically target and do their business when these major markets centers are open at the same time. This brief overlap in the time zones of the markets result in the most active market times for trading.

Unfortunately one of the downsides that most novice traders will come across in Forex is that there is a high learning curve. This often means that it will take a while before the novice trader gains the experience and knowledge necessary to enjoy the full prosperity of the Forex market and their investments. Luckily this is no longer the case. Expert traders are now willing to share their advice, knowledge, and help beginning Forex trader's understand the market and make lots of money.

FOREX MARKET OPEN TIMES - WHAT YOU NEED TO KNOW

Forex trading is one of the fastest growing ways of making money through the internet, and forex market open times are one of the reasons for this. There is a huge capacity for making money from the comfort of your own home and generating an income that keeps all the profits for you. If you are interested in getting into forex marketing, then there is a lot of information that you need to know to increase your chances of being successful.

Forex trading stands for foreign exchange trading. Basically, this means that you are trading currencies and making profits off the gains in currency as the market around the world ebbs and flows.

One of the reasons that this style of internet work is becoming so popular is that it is a 24 hour market, so it really does not matter where in the world you live or what working hours would you want to set. The market is open 5 and a half days of the week, starting out in Australia on a Sunday evening and closing in New York on a Friday night.

Forex market open times are usually between 8am and 4pm in the country where they are operating. However, you can find markets open at any time somewhere in the world in order to do your trading. Even though you can trade at any time, it is best to trade when there is the highest concentration of trades going on.

This next point is an important one for people who are new to forex. It is usually best to trade when the three biggest markets are open, that is: London, New York and Tokyo. The reason is that most fluctuations and activities are going to take place when these markets are operating.

The most action occurs when there are two markets that are open simultaneously, and this is when you want to kick into action and make some trades yourself. You can find time converters online, which can tell you when the markets around the world are open for trading.

Forex trading is a great way to earn yourself income from the comfort of your own home. If you are considering getting into this market, then there is plenty to learn about to ensure that you get the profits that you are after. Knowing how to work with the forex market open times is an important part of ensuring your overall success in the market.

FOREX MARKET OPEN TIMES - TAKE ADVANTAGE OF THEM

If you are just getting into the world of forex trading, then knowing about the forex market open times is an important part of ensuring you get the results that you are looking for. This style of internet based work is now so common because there is a massive capacity for making profits if you understand the way it works and learn as much as you can about the market.

Forex trading is short for foreign exchange trading and it deals with making profits off the trades that you make in pairs of currency. To be successful, you need to keep up to date with the market and be able to identify trends in the market.

The forex market is operational 24 hours a day, for five and a 1/2 days each week. It opens in Australia on Sunday night and it closes in New York on Friday evening. This means that you can make trades at any time in this window time. However, there are some strategies that you need to be aware of.

Forex market open times generally are between 8 in the morning until 4 in the afternoon in the country that the market is based in. This means that you can find markets that are open any time around the world in order to do your trading. Even though you are able to trade at any point in the day, it is best to trade when there is the highest concentration of trades going on.
In general, it is best to make your trades when one of the three largest markets is open for trading. The three biggest markets are

London, Tokyo and New York. You want to trade during these times because that this is the period of time in which there is the most movement in exchange rates and therefore the most money to be made.

There is even more action taking place when two markets are operating at the same time. This is when you really want to be sitting up and taking notice of what is going on. There are time converters for forex trading available online, which can help you identify when markets are open and closed.

Getting into forex trading is a potentially very profitable business. The key to being successful is to understand the system and the way that everything works.

Understanding how to work together with the forex market open time to maximize your results can help you become profitable more quickly and see impressive results for your work.

FOREX MARKET OPEN TIMES - HOW TO BENEFIT OFF IT

Trading the foreign exchange market is now a very common way of earning an income from the comfort of your home office. And one of the keys to being successful is understanding about the forex market open times. If you want to get great results from your forex trading efforts, then understanding the ways that you can maximize your efforts is very important. Forex trading is the short version for foreign exchange trading. What this means is that you make profits from selling one foreign currency or buying others. You normally trade in the top eight currencies in the world, which includes the British pound, US dollar, Japanese Yen, Canadian, Australian & New Zealand dollars, the Euro, and the Swiss franc.

The market that you work within is open 24 hours a day as the world markets are all open at differing times. This means that regardless of where you live, you can participate and earn profits on your trades. The market is open from Sunday night in Australia to Friday night in New York and it closes over the weekend. Forex market open times are generally from eight in the morning until four in the afternoon in each particular country. While it is possible to trade at any time in 24 hours, the best times to trade are usually when there is the highest concentration of trading happening, as this is when you see the biggest gains.

The highest concentration of trades generally occurs when the biggest markets are open, and that means Tokyo, New York, and London. Therefore it is usually best if you are ready to trade when these markets are open and operational.

To really maximize your profits, it is even better to trade when more than one market is open at a time. There is really dynamic action that happens then. In order to work out when this is occurring, you can use time converters online, which show when markets around the world are open or shut.

Forex trading is really taking off as a way for people to either earn themselves a living income or a bit of extra pocket money. How it will work for you depends on the time that you put into understanding the system and the way that foreign exchange works. To make sure that you get the best results you can, you need to understand how to make the forex market open times work for you.

THE BEST TIME TO TRADE THE FOREX MARKET

The one thing that marks a forex market is its dynamic nature. Here fortunes change in seconds and minutes. If taken positively, this feature also allows a trader to enter the market many times in a single day and garner some profit for himself.

Timing is one thing that would actually determine your success in the forex market and that is why it is essential to find the best time to trade the forex market, the best time with regards to activity, volume of trade etc.

There are some salient features of forex market and until and unless these are understood one cannot find out the best time to trade the forex market. Forex markets work 24 hours. It starts from Sunday 5 pm EST through Friday 4 pm EST and rollovers at 5 pm EST. Forex trading starts from New Zealand and then is followed by Australia, Asia, the Middle East, Europe and America. The most prominent forex market is undoubtedly the US and the UK. They account for more than half of the total market transactions.

If it comes to major forex markets, London, New York and Tokyo would win hands down. Around 75% of market activities in the New York markets are witnessed in the morning hours while the European markets are still open. And if you want to know when the forex trading is the heaviest, well look for the time when the major markets overlap.

One thing must be evident from this discussion. There is never a cease down in the forex market. When its day for you, its night for someone else. Markets close somewhere and simultaneously, markets open somewhere else. That is what offers traders this tremendous opportunity to make some serious money.

Forex market is characterized by high liquidity and high flexibility and as such traders get the freedom to make choices as per their wishes. They are not bound by the whims of the markets.

So, when you try to determine the best time to trade the forex market this information would prove very useful. Trades have almost always the same relative frequency and until the forex market remains open, the probability of finding a trade whenever you look is almost the same. This is all about volume of trade. It is determined by the number of markets that are open and the number of times each of these markets overlap with each other.

Keeping in mind the forex volume is extremely essential. It is generally seen that the volume of transactions remains high all through the day but when does it peak? The answer is when the Asian markets with Australia and New Zealand, the European markets and the US markets open simultaneously. This is the best time to trade the forex market.

Let's have a look of the timings of some of these markets.

- *New York Market : 8 am - 4 pm EST*
- *London Market : 2 am - 12 noon EST*
- *Great Britain Market : 3 am - 11 am EST*
- *Tokyo Market : 8 pm - 4 am EST*
- *Australian Market : 7 pm - 3 pm EST*

Just have a look at the above schedule carefully. What do you see? Yes, there are two times when two of the major markets overlap during the trading hours-between 2 am and 4 am EST (Asian/Europe) and between 8 am to 12 pm EST (European/N. American). This is the time you have to target to make profits, the best time to trade the forex markets.

The forex trading is open at all times throughout the business week. The forex market hours span from Monday morning (Sydney time) to

Friday afternoon (New York time). At any given moment during that interval, it is open somewhere in the world.

In order to find out the exact forex market hours, one should be familiar with the various time zones. This is very simple once you express them in correlation with the Universal Coordinated Time (UTC) - also widely known as the Greenwich Mean Time (GMT). This is the "base" time zone throughout the world, as it is the standard winter time at the point of zero longitude. As such, the forex market hours are from 22:00 Sunday to 22:00 Friday, according to the base time zone. In New York time, trading opens at 5 p.m. on Sundays and closes at 5 p.m. on Fridays; in U.S. west coast time, its 2 p.m.; in Germany time, its 11 p.m. and in Sydney time 8 a.m.

It's a bit more complex when the daylight saving time gets factored in; as the change doesn't occur at the same time all over the globe, a difference of one hour appears as some countries observe the change. Also, the daylight saving is different in the southern hemisphere - summer time from September to March, opposite to the northern hemisphere (March to September).

There are four major national markets in the world. Their forex market hours are 1 p.m. to 10 p.m. UTC (8 a.m. to 5 p.m. EST) for New York, 8 a.m. to 5 p.m. UTC (3 a.m. to 12 noon EST) for London, 10 p.m. to 7 a.m UTC (5 p.m. to 2 a.m. EST) for Sydney and 12 midnight to 9 a.m. UTC (7 p.m. to 4 a.m. EST) for Tokyo. Together, these markets cover the entire 24 hours of any given business day.

Although it is open throughout the day, there are certain periods when the prices become unpredictable; this generally happens when a major market opens for the day. At these times, many traders choose to stop making any transactions until it becomes stable again.

The most traded currency in the world is the U.S. dollar. Statistics show that this currency is used in trades 2.5 times more often than the Euro, the second most often used currency. Because of this, the U.S. market is the most influential in the world. Also, if you are involved in trading U.S. dollars, the best time to stop trading for the day is around 8 p.m. UTC (3 p.m. EST), as that is the time when New York begins to slow down. While the forex market hours makes it possible to trade 24 hours a day (especially with the aid of automated software), most traders will choose the best times to trade instead of being active at all times.

WHAT TIME DOES FOREX MARKET CLOSE AROUND THE WORLD?

If you are new to forex trading, then you might be wondering about a number of things, such as what time does forex market close around the world? There is much to know in order to get the best results that you can from your trades and be able to turn a reliable and consistent profit.

Forex trading deals with buying and selling foreign currencies for profit. You always deal in pairs of currencies and usually you will be buying and selling the eight top currencies, which include: the Japanese yen, the British pound, Swiss francs, US, Australian, Canadian and New Zealand dollars and the euro.

It is important that you know what time the markets around the globe open and close in order to maximize your profits and minimize the chances of losses. You can trade at any time of the day from Sunday night, when the Aussie market opens, through Friday night when the New York market comes to a close.

What time does forex market close, is a two fold answer. On the one hand you can find forex markets open at any point during the day between the aforementioned times between Sydney and New York. However, the markets in each country generally open at 8am and close at 4pm in the time zone of the respective market.
If you trade when one of the big three markets is open and operational, then you are likely to get the highest gains as this is when there is the most action between the exchange rates of the currencies. The big three are the New York, Tokyo and London markets.

If you are unsure about what times these markets are open in relation to the specific time zone that you live in, then you can find time converters online to help you out. They can help you work out when different markets are open or closed at any point in time.

It is important to try and make trades when the biggest markets are operational, but you can get even better results if there is more than one market open at a time. A timing converter can give you this information as well and make getting bigger and better profits more regularly for you. Knowing the ins and outs of the forex trading business means that you will have a more reliable result for your trades and knowing what time does the forex market close at any given time is a vital part of that.

CHAPTER 4

FOREX PAIRS

Forex pairs trading is a great deal easier when you've got the right tools and information. This is where forex trading software comes into play. 25% of all traders were recently estimated to be using forex trading software in one form or another because of the ease or accuracy it brings to their campaigns.

Because the forex market keeps much longer hours than the traditional stock exchange, you've got to be able to stay on top of the market at all times to truly be successful. It's just common sense. While this can be next to impossible, forex trading software was designed to take a lot of the weight and burden off of the average trader in their forex pairs trading. Stop loss and take profit protocols help to ensure that you'll be on the winning side of all of your trades the vast majority of the time. If the market ever quickly changes out of your favor, the forex software snaps into action and trades away to minimize your losses.

There is a great deal of human error associated with making quick decisions in forex pairs trading, but it's necessary at the same time. Not only have you got to be able to decide that a certain trade is the right and best move, you've got to do it in a time limit of a very short period to truly monetize on your decision. Forex software does this for you at all hours of every day and all for the one time fee when you first buy the system. If you hired someone to do it for you it would quickly begin to cost you a fortune.

To get the best results from your forex pairs trading, you need the best information guiding your trading. The best signals or tips to guide your trading come from the signal generators in forex trading software. These programs use complex mathematical algorithms to constantly analyze the market and its trends and changes to generate the most accurate tips of where it's going next. There is no substitute for forex trading software if you want the most accurate information guiding your forex pairs trading. Many traders swear by the tips they receive from these programs.

A currency pair is another way of looking at exchange rates between two different currencies. Two currencies are used to give a ratio of value based on the conversion of one currency into the other. They are comprised of two parts - the base currency and the counter currency - but there is no better way of exploring this than looking at an example!

EUR/USD 1.240

Above you will see the currency pair known as the "Fibre." More on why it is called a fibre later..! Firstly we can see that there are two currencies involved - the Euro and the American Dollar. The above pretty much says the following:

"1 unit of the base currency Euro will get you 1.24 units of the counter currency USD."

Pretty simple! The base currency is the Euro and the counter currency is the American dollar. When we trade 1 Euro we expect to get 1.24 dollars based on the ratio/quotation. If the quote changes to 1.26 then the Euro has increased in relative value. If the quote drops to 1.22 then the Euro has slipped in value.

Whilst the concept is simple the formulation of currency pairs still falls to quite a stringent structure. There are rules for forming a currency pair although they are more an established priority list rather than set by a body or organisation.

Historically they were the result of ranking according to relative value with respect to one another however the introduction of the Euro changed the formulation. In 1999 the European Central Bank ensured that the Euro would have first precedence as a base currency when used in a currency pair. As such the priority list goes a little something like this...

- euro
- pound sterling
- Australian dollar
- New Zealand dollar
- United States dollar
- Canadian dollar
- Swiss franc
- Japanese Yen

Usually currency pairs are created in a hierarchical order - for example when talking about the rate between the USD and Canadian dollar you would use the following: USD/CAD 1.04. Or if looking for a pair of Australian dollar to British pound you would use GBP/AUD 1.59. The base currency is dictated by the hierarchy. The most widely used currency pairs are known as "Majors" and include the following currency pairs.

- EUR/USD
- UR/USD
- GBP/USD
- AUD/USD
- USD/CHF

Other currencies (the Minors) are generally quoted against one of the major currencies. Currency pairs that do not involve the USD are known as cross currency pairs with the exception of Euro pairs which are known as Euro Crosses.

By now I'm sure you are thinking about how to use these new found pairs in general conversation or shock horror in a trade conversation. There are three additional terms to think about - the spot rate (usually the rate of exchange based on the pair for that given moment in time), the spread and the pip. The spread and the pip are terms used by the forex trader. During a trade a currency is often offered at a sale price or "ask price" - the trader then puts in a "bid" price based which they hope is lower than the ask. The difference between the two rates is known as "the spread" and the quantity is known as a "pip". If the pair quote for GBP/USD is 1.5709 at the bid rate but 1.5704 then the spread is 0.0005 GBP or 5 pips. Ideally you want to get as many pips as possible. Trading in large quantities is thus important when making money from trades but can obviously present some associated risks! Unsurprisingly a "bureau de change" makes their money from exchanges like this by ensuring the spread is wide. So why is EUR/USD called a "fibre"? Some say that "fibre" probably follows the trend of other currency pair nicknames like the GBP/USD's "cable" moniker. Cable was derived from the way in which data was transferred between the two countries (i.e. a huge cable under the Atlantic Ocean that synchronized the GBP/USD quote). It is quite possible that fibre reflects the fibre optic age of communications. Forex trading is based on currency pairs. You cannot enter a trade with a single currency. You need to work on its demand/supply imbalance against some other currency. This is where forex trading becomes an entity requiring a currency pair. There are many pairs and its liquid derivatives. EUR/USD, USD/JPY, GBP/CHF, NZD/USD are a few of its kind.

Imbalance in demand or supply of a currency and moreover, its floating near its stable mark or far from it, causes it to rise or fall. Forex trading pair is the least regulated market and provides great leverage and liquidity to its traders. You buy a currency and sell the other. This introduces an exchange rate. If you get the better of the exchange rates and trade a currency on a high, you will make money. You will lose in a contrary situation.

Let's take an example. A trader can buy Japanese Yen with dollars. If the Yen rises against dollars, he can sell his portfolio and make profit out of it. If Yen loses steam, a trader can look to hedge the same portfolio or try to hedge it through buying a different portfolio. For this instance, it can be buying US dollar against a moderate EURO.

While trading in forex pairs, there is always a base currency and a counter currency. Base currency has a one unit standard value. For instance, in case of USD/EUR, you can look to buy .7 EUR with 1 USD. Here, we are using USD as the base currency; generally, a trader trades in 1, 00,000 units of a base currency.

If you need money now, like I mean in the next hour, try what I did. I am making more money now than in my old business and you can too, read the amazing, true story, in the link below. When I joined I was skeptical for just ten seconds before I realized what this was. I was smiling from ear to ear and you will too. Imagine doubling your money every week with no or little risk! To discover a verified list of Million Dollar Corporations offering you their products at 75% commission to you. Click the link below to learn HOW you will begin compounding your capital towards your first Million Dollars at the easy corporate money program.

If you're involved with currency trading, you obviously know what forex pairs are. The pair is the two currencies that are currently involved in your trade. So lets take US dollars and Swiss francs as an example, if you're trading those two currencies the pair is USD/CHF. It's possible to trade any two currencies of the world, but that's a bright idea really, as you need to be trading two currencies that have larger financial powers. It doesn't necessarily mean that you should be trading currencies of two of the most powerful countries. Switzerland is a major currency when it comes to forex trading, even though it's only a relatively small country. The reason why it's a big player in the forex world, is because the Swiss bank are important globally.

Below are the 6 most popular forex pairs, they account for 90% of trades on the forex market. They are:

* EUR/USD - The Euro and the US Dollar.
* GBP/USD - The British Pound and the US Dollar
* USD/JPY - The US Dollar and the Japanese Yen
* USD/CHF - The US Dollar and the Swiss Franc
* AUD/USD - The Australian Dollar and the US Dollar
* USD/CAD - The US Dollar and the Canadian Dollar

It's quite rare that traders get involved with other currencies, but the most experienced traders do tend to trade different pairs from time to time, which usually involves the New Zealand Dollar. If you're just starting out it's vital that you stick with the major forex pairs.

The US is the most popular currency when it comes to trading, it's involved in 85% of all trades according to the latest study. The Euro is the second most popular at 37%. Next follow the Yen, Pound, Franc, AUD and CAD.

WHAT IS THE BEST CURRENCY PAIR FOR A BEGINNER?

There is a lot of information online about trading with the EUR/USD pair. Seriously, there is a lot of valuable information out there that you can use to start trading with this currency pair. Experts recommend beginner's start out with trading this popular forex pair, due to the wealth of information available online.

If you're just starting out you definitely want to stick with EUR/USD. If, for whatever reason, you don't want to stick with that, then I recommend you trade the GBP/USD pair.

TYPES OF FOREX PAIRS

Most people know that currency pairs are traded in pairs, and a trader can make a profit as one currency's value changes against another. But which currency pairs to trade? And what are the differences between them?

Currency pairs fall into three categories - majors, crosses and exotics.

MAJOR FOREX PAIRS

Major forex pairs are pairs that consist of a major currency and the US dollar, such as:

- AUD/USD - Australian and US dollars
- EUR/USD - Euro and US dollar
- GBP/USD - British pound and US dollar
- NZD/USD - New Zealand and US dollars
- USD/CAD - US and Canadian dollars
- USD/CHF - US dollar and Swiss franc
- USD/JPY - US dollar and Japanese Yen

Some features of the major forex pairs include:

- Many of the major forex pairs move in similar patterns - for example, the EUR/USD and GBP/USD usually move in the same direction, so if one is moving up or down, it is likely that the other will follow the same trend, though the GBP/USD is a bit more volatile.

- As the CHF is another European currency, it also moves in correlation with the EUR and GBP. As the major currency pair is USD/CHF (the US dollar being the first named currency), this means that it will move in negative correlation with the EUR/USD and GBP/USD, so it will trend in the opposite direction.

The EUR/USD is the most widely traded pair, making up about 27% of total trading volume, so it is also the most liquid of the major currency pairs. It is also the pair that many beginners feel most comfortable with - due to its liquidity it is possible to profit in short time frames, which is cheaper as you won't have as many interest charges, and there is constantly information available about this pair online and in the news.

COMMODITY CURRENCIES

A commodity currency is the currency of a country that depends heavily on the export of raw minerals for income the Australian, Canadian and New Zealand dollars are considered to be both major and commodity currencies.

FOREX CROSSES

A cross is a pair of currencies that does not include the US dollar, such as:

- AUD/CAD - Australian and Canadian dollars
- AUD/CHF - Australian dollar and Swiss franc
- AUD/JPY - Australian dollar and Japanese yen
- AUD/NZD - Australian and New Zealand dollars
- CAD/JPY - Canadian dollar and Japanese yen
- CHF/JPY - Swiss franc and Japanese yen
- EUR/AUD - Euro and Australian dollar
- EUR/CAD - Euro and Canadian dollar
- EUR/CHF - Euro and Swiss franc
- EUR/GBP - Euro and British pound
- EUR/JPY - Euro and Japanese yen
- EUR/NZD - Euro and New Zealand dollar
- GBP/AUD - British pound and Australian dollar
- GBP/CHF - British pound and Swiss franc

- GBP/CZK - British pound and Czech crown
- GBP/JPY - British pound and Japanese yen
- NZD/JPY - New Zealand dollar and Japanese yen

The most watched crosses are AUD/JPY, EUR/JPY, GBP/JPY and NZD/JPY.

EXOTIC FOREX PAIRS

Exotic forex pairs are currency pairs that comprise currencies of developing and emerging economies, such as:
- USD/TRY - US dollar and Turkish lira
- EUR/TRY - Euro and Turkish lira
- USD/ZAR - US dollar and South African rand
- USD/MXN - US dollar and Mexican peso
- USD/SGD - US dollar and Singapore dollar

It isn't usually recommended that beginners start trading in exotic forex pairs for a number of reasons:

1. Exotics are much less liquid than major pairs, which means they have wider bid/offer spreads (a spread is the difference between the buy and the sell price - the wider this is, the more you need a currency to move to make a profit) than the major forex pairs.

2. When exotics do move, they can be very volatile and unpredictable.

3. here is less information available about these pairs than the major currency pairs, or even crosses.

It is usually best to start trading with a couple of forex pairs at a time, and build a winning strategy before adding more currency pairs to your portfolio.

f you want to be able to effectively trade the Forex, then you need to understand how Forex pairs work. "Forex pairs" is another way of saying "currency pair." All trading in the Forex market is done not with individual currencies, but with currency pairs. To trade the U.S. Dollar (USD) you have to choose another currency to trade it against. This is why understanding Forex pairs is so important. It's not enough to understand one currency. You have to understand how two currencies are going to relate to one another.

The major currencies, and major currency pairs, will account for nearly 80-85% of all Forex trades world wide. The reasons for this are fairly simple and straight forward. The strongest economies are often the most stable and come from the most stable governments. This security and strength of economy is what makes these main currencies strongest and the best to trade.

Look at Zimbabwe's hyperinflation as a reason why smaller nations and nations with dictators aren't trusted in currency trading. There are too many variables, and an economy can completely change overnight. Governments that operate by Democracy and that are strong aren't likely to fold. Economies given freedom to operate on their own also tend to work in a stable way. Even the most unstable weeks or months in the United States would have less effect on the currency than if China's leadership decided to shut out all foreign investment tomorrow.

This is part of the reason China's currency hasn't broken into the major players, while nations like Canada and New Zealand have.

While it's unlikely that China would have a sudden shift like this, it is possible. That type of insecurity is why China's Yuan isn't going to be in position to stand up with the CAD, NZD, or CHF any time soon.
The most common Forex pairs will get traded the most because the Forex market is volatile enough without the dangers of governments shutting down foreign investment, military coups, or any of the other common worries associated with these nations.

Russia fighting Georgia, China cracking down on dissent, India and Pakistan - even modern developed nations can be too unstable for good currency strength.
So when you're looking for a good currency pair to trade, don't get cute with Yuans, Pesos, or Rubles, but stay with the big dogs. They provide all the profit opportunity that a good Forex trader needs.

How Forex Pair Correlations Affect Your Trading

Forex pair correlations may seem daunting, but a basic understanding of correlations can go a long way toward helping you to become a better trader.

In fact, not understanding forex pair correlations when trading can be disastrous, but by learning a bit more about correlations many pitfalls can be avoided... and possibly some additional strategies can be added to your forex trading arsenal.

What are Forex Pair Correlations?

A correlation is a measure moves with another. Correl of how much one currency ations will run between -100 and +100, the former meaning they move in exactly the opposite direction, and the latter indicating they move in the same direction.

Assume you wish to know the correlation of the EUR/USD to the GBP/USD. Quite often these pairs will move in a similar fashion, although not exactly. If two pairs moves in a similar way they will have a + correlation. Therefore, the EUR/USD and GBP/USD may have a +70 correlation on an hourly time frame, +83 on a daily time frame and +86 on a weekly time frame.

When pairs move the opposite direction, they will have a (negative) correlation. The EUR/USD and USD/CHF are often negatively correlated, and therefore may have a -87 correlation on the daily time frame for example.

A +100 correlation means two pairs moves exactly the same. A -100 correlation means the pairs move exactly opposite. A correlation of 0 (zero) or a small + or - number means the pairs have no real correlation and if they do move together it is more likely to be random than anything significant. Therefore, a correlation of +35 or -41 means for the most part the pairs do not have a strong correlation.

Correlations will change all the time, but it is important to be aware of them. The statistics on the Daily Forex Statistics are updated daily to reflect current forex pair correlations. The correlations are presented in a matrix as shown in the figure below, and are presented for hourly, daily and weekly data.

HOW TO USE FOREX PAIR CORRELATION DATA

Here are a couple examples of how you can use forex pair correlation in your trading, to manage risk or hedge positions.

If you have multiple positions that are highly correlated (positive value over 70) it means that the pairs move somewhat in tandem. This means you may be overexposed to one currency, even though the risk on each position is managed. For example if you are long the EUR/USD and long the GBP/USD, you may be risking more than you expect since the pairs are highly correlated. Same for if you are long the EUR/USD and short the USD/CHF. These pairs are often inversely correlated, so by being long one and short the other, once again this may expose you to more risk than anticipated since if one trade loses the other is likely to as well.

You can hedge a trade in one currency pair with a trade in another that has a high (above 80) number. Go long the EUR/USD and you can hedge with a short position in the GBP/USD; since the pairs are positively correlated positions much be taken in opposite directions (long and short). For strong inverse correlations, both postions must be the same to form the hedge, such as long and long, or short and short.

Just because two pairs are highly negatively or positively correlated does not mean they will "offset" each others losses when hedging. Since each pair may move a different amount (more or less volatile), volatility is another factor which must be considered when looking at hedging.

CHAPTER 5

WHERE WE TRADE FOREX?

The forex market can be a very profitable place for someone who understands how to begin trading and more importantly where to begin trading at. There are many online forex trading platforms on the internet today that claim to offer the best services and most advantages for trading. I can tell you that many of them are not top of the line and will not help traders begin the best trading platform that one can find on the internet today will offer the best known software available with an easy registration on start up. Along with this software will come many other advantages such as high deposit bonuses, good leverage, good training tools, and great customer support. Only few have all these services and more.

eToro is probably the most prestige trading platform available to traders today. It offers all of the above
services and allows new traders a quick and easy start up. You will first see that there website and their software is top of the line and they will help all traders get started and learn how to b profitable in their trading. Also eToro offers up to $1000 bonuses on first time deposits.
Another good choice of trading platform is Forex Place or also known as 4XP. Even though they may not be quite as highly ranked as eToro they are still at great trading platform for any user that is looking to get into the forex market. Their software and support both are one of the best and they also offer good bonuses and training tools along the way.

The last place that will be mentioned here is 10Pips trading platform. It is another highly esteemed forex broker and is used by many traders today. 10Pips offers many great benefits along with a good software program and good leverage for their traders. This allows the possibility to make a whole lot of money in just a little bit of time.

Do not be fooled by many platforms out there that do not give you the quality, the training, or the support as these and some others. If you are looking to get into the forex market and do well in it, make sure you pick the right place to trade.

Foreign exchange trading or Forex which is commonly known is where traders from all around the world trade financial instruments such as currency and stocks online.

HOW DOES IT WORKS?

Let us take the case of Japan Yen with The US Dollars. You use your Japan Yen to trade for US Dollars and you can earn money through the arbitraging of the currency.

WHO ARE THE PARTIES INVOLVED IN THE FOREIGN EXCHANGE MARKETS?

The parties that are involved in the forex markets include huge local banks from different countries, government related investment bodies, large multi-national businesses and financial institutions such as pension funds,private banks and insurance companies.

It works when there are two parties,one party consisting of the the investor and the other is the country where the money is being invested in by the investor. Normally, the trade is done through a financial intermediaries such as the bank who acts as the broker to enable smooth transaction between the two party. This is just the minuscule of forex.

A forex market trade can be commenced as long as there are at least two or more parties involving in the deal and it takes place worldwide with millions of traders from different countries doing trades.

HOW BIG IS THE FOREX MARKET?

The foreign exchange market is made up of multiple parties trading in the Forex market large volumes of assets and large amounts of money which may amounts to millions at one time. The parties that participate in the forex market are generally those involving in business involving cash or doing trades of very liquidable assets that you can sell and buy fast. The market therefore acts like a meeting place for them to deal.

The forex market as you have understand is much larger than the stock market in any one country as it involves all the forex traders in the world gathering in one centralised market to do deal.
Even when you are reading this article now,there are traders in the Forex market that are trading and you can say that trading takes place

24 hours daily but do take note that the forex market is done usually during weekdays although there are times that traders may close their deals udring the weekend.

Just imagine the sheer number of traders that amounts to millions dealing with forex and you have an impression on the cash pot in forex

HOW MUCH IS THE FOREX INDUSTRY WORTH?

As of a research and statistic recorded in the late 2004,there are close to two trillion dollars (that is two million million!) was traded on a daily basis. This is an astronomical number for compared to stock markets and think of the number of daily transactions that takes place. With so much cash flowing in the forex market daily, it is not surprised that people have gave up their daily job to trade daily on forex market as there are so much cash to be earned through it.

The forex market has been around for more than 20 years and has been done in a brick and mortar manner but with the accessiblity of the computer and the internet, the forex trading continues to grow increasing and has taken to another level as more individual traders and smallers businesses trade online because of the ease and security that allows them to trade

CAN I TRADE FOREX ONLINE?

You might be surprised that trading Forex online is as easy as just a few clicks away on your mouse and anyone is able to trade as long as you have the basic knowledge of Forex.

The best thing is that opening an online forex account is totally Free. Just recently,there is the article that a Japanese housewife won over 5 million dollars throughout her Forex investing adventure for about 10 years with minimal capital. How did she do that? By trading forex online.

If a housewife can do it,with just a little knowledge, I am sure you cant see why you can't do it. Now you must be thinking, where to trade forex?
10 Things I Wish I Had Known Before I Started Trading Forex

Are you thinking about trying your hand at forex? Think you might have what it takes to be successful? Don't fall in the same traps that so many before you have fallen into. Taken from successful and yet-to-be successful traders from all over the world, and some from my own book of forex blunders, here are 10 things most wish they'd known before they started to trade foreign exchange. And if I may be so bold, print this out and hang it right beside your computer monitor!

1. Make Money with a Practice Account First. Don't trade a single penny of your own money until
you've had ample experience with a practice account. I first started trading forex in college and thought I was smarter than the hundreds of people who had failed before me. I did open a practice account,

but apparently thought I was ready to trade for real after a short three days. I've come along way since then, but that mistake cost me a small fortune to a college student. It translated into many missed nights out with my friends as I slowly tried to recoup what I had lost. Had I known what I do now I would have used a practice account for a month or more, gotten confident with my strategy, and wouldn't have lost track of orders that should have been cancelled because they were no longer valid. You won't make money during that time, but you won't lose money either, and that is half the battle. You'll find that out soon enough the hard way if you don't heed this important advice.

2. Trading With Real Money is Different. As much as opening a practice account is good, trading with real money on the line is different. Try as you might to trade the same way with real money as you did with pretend money, the reality is that it just isn't the same when you've actually got something at stake. Seeing your account increase or decrease with each pip can be taken in stride when playing for fun, but can be excruciating when it's your money on the table. One way that helped me get over this was to think of each trade as the cost of doing business. For example, a business might spend money on an ad which is either going to make them money or it's not. Either way, the money spent on the ad is gone, so you should have done your research before spending the money to determine whether or not it was a good idea. It's much the same with forex. When you place a trade with a stoploss, consider the money at risk the cost of doing business. If you are not prepared to lose it, then you need to think twice about taking the trade in the first place.

3. Forex is a Mental Game. There is a psychology to trading. There are mental and emotional states that can help your trading, and ones that can be
extremely detrimental. You don't trade if you have been put-off by a loss and are looking for vindication, nor do you trade when you've come off a win and you think you are invisible. You don't trade when

you are bored and you've got an itchy trigger finger, nor when you are tired, having a bad day, and especially not when you are thinking about how much you need the money. Trading with dollar signs in you eyes will result in taking trades that you shouldn't. Mindsets like these are a recipe for disaster. I thought I was a pretty even keel, more pragmatic than most, and level-headed. I didn't think I was going to be vulnerable to the emotional side of the game. Here's what I wish someone had told me: Expect to be emotional, but know that not keeping your emotions in check will be your demise.

4. Don't Lament the One that Got Away. Don't sit on the sidelines watching some grand move in the market wishing you were in the trade. Chances are you'll convince yourself to get in and you will get burned. It's like trying to catch a falling knife; let it fall. Watching a pair make a big move that you missed is hard. Expect it to be. It sucks. But watching the pair go and thinking about getting in is like trying to cross a one-way street by looking the wrong way. Watching cars go by and seeing big gaps in traffic where you could have crossed provides no insight as to when you can cross. Just because you are looking at a painful gap in traffic that was definitely would have given you ample time, doesn't mean there's not a transport isn't yards away. Train yourself to look the other way.

Look at what's coming, the set ups that are developing, not the ones that already developed. Begin to recognize when you are looking the wrong way down the Forex street, and force yourself to think differently.

5. Plan the Trade, Trade the Plan. Have a trading plan before you press that buy or sell button.
Know at what price you'd like to get in at, how much you are willing to risk, and where you'd like to see the price go. Know why you are taking a trade, and understand why your stoploss and target price are where they are. If you don't know why you are taking a trade, or don't know ho wot plan a trade, then you've got more learning to do.

Just be sure to have a really clear understanding of your trading strategy before you begin.

6. Have Respect for the Profession. Professional traders spend years in school, have mentors and work with other professionals in the field, and have the most advance tools and software at their finger tips to help them perfect the skill of trading foreign exchange. Don't expect after a month or two of trading that you know even a fraction of what these guys know. If you think you've got it all figured out how you can make a million dollars in the next three months on forex, think again. Trading forex takes some humility. You are a tiny fish in a big pond. Did you know that professional traders have a track record that usually just above 50 percent? That means they make winning trades approximately (on average) between 5 or 6 times for every 10 trades they make. That is because of what is called trade management. Stoplosses and targets are intelligently placed so that while they may lose 50 pips on a losing trade, they make 150 on a winning one. If you can do that 50% of the time you are making money. Don't waltz into the forex world thinking you can change the game, or be that one in a million that can make a few uninformed choices and you get lucky. Don't think you've got it all figured out or have an edge on the guys who make a career out of doing this. It's that slow and steady that wins the race.

7. It's All About the Trades You Don't Make. Be a trading snob. Once you understand the basics of any given trading strategy (there are many), be a picky trader. Trade only when all your criterion for taking a trade are met. A big part of trading forex successfully is knowing when not to trade. I can't emphasize this point enough. To be successful at forex you have to first not lose your money, and that means staying out of losing trades. Make staying out of losing trades a priority, this goes back again to being a picky trader.

8. Don't Be a Maverick, Be a Follower. To make money in forex you need to be doing what everybody else is doing, when they are doing it. It's not the time to re-invent the wheel, or get ahead of the curve. That will only result in lost pips. It doesn't matter what you know about currency, or the state of a country's economy. What matters is what the market is actually doing, not what it should be doing. Trying to find the bottom or top of a huge move or a trend is more like gambling than trading. If you are tempted to trade like this, do yourself a favour and go to Vegas where at least you can enjoy free drinks and catch a few shows while you lose your money. It's not a good sign if you are trying to time the markets. If you are, you are in need of an intervention. Don't bother placing the trade; take out the middle man and just send a big fat cheque directly to your online broker. The goal is not to get in when the market has bottomed. The goal is to get in when there is solid evidence that the market is going to go in a particular direction. That is rarely 10, or even 100 pips from the low. The key is to get in when there are indicators that it will go, not when you think its' the bottom.

9. You're Going to Be Glued to Your Computer. At least chances are you will be. And I am not saying that's a good thing. Just know that this is a real possibility as you try to make money. It's easy to become obsessed with watching the markets, looking for opportunities, and making trades, smart ones and stupid ones. While it is important to put in face time, watch the markets and do analysis, if you are making smart trades you should essentially be able to make a trade and walk away and be OK with whatever happens. Be aware that it's easy to become a slave to forex. Take measures against becoming one by educating yourself on a trading style and strategy that you are comfortable with so that you don't fall that trap.

10. Don't Just Learn, Get Help. It's just not enough to read about trading forex or to take a course, free or otherwise. If you want to implement a strategy effectively, it's simple: Get help. Learning

and knowing what to do is not enough. You need the help and experience of a forex expert. There are some decent seminars and coaching programs that are available for free, but a good coach is money well spent. It's as close to getting your hand held as it gets. Quality membership sites and coaching programs can cost as little as $50 a month, to well over $200.

CHAPTER 6

CHOOSING A BROKER

The forex broker will be the absolute key to your success on the forex market. Without the support of your broker you will find it much more time to understand the market and to actually make money, and as such you should always be looking for certain key requirements when it comes to any forex brokers who might interest you.

Opening a forex trading account is a task that requires nerves of steel, especially for those, not familiar with the system. You might have heard about several Forex cons that caused individuals to lose their hard-earned money all because they fell prey to unreliable and fake brokers. Fraudsters such as these generally register their company as singular official foreign exchange brokers. They encourage potential clients to open accounts through them and then eventually embezzle the deposited funds.

With such brokers, it is not uncommon to be denied access to one's hard-earned cash. Once a client requests withdrawal of funds, after having opened an account, the broker refuses to honor the request.

These fraudsters totally ignore the request or find various reasons to withhold the cash. Sometimes, they simply close the account. This usually happens with those who do not live in the country or region where the broker is registered. Otherwise, one would have a chance to sue them and file a petition for the fraud committed.

As the online Forex trading market becomes increasingly saturated and the choice of brokers becomes wider, the decision of which broker to run with becomes increasingly important for the trader. Although the majority of brokers provide the same basic trading platform, there can be a vast difference in what they offer their clients, both in terms of trading conditions as well as customer support. By simply visiting a company's homepage it may be hard to separate the second-rate firms from the professionals, therefore this chapter will examine the main parameters that should be taken into consideration before creating an account and depositing.

For those seeking to start up a new Forex account, below is a guide that will assist them in avoiding the pitfalls and finding the right broker.

COMPARE ON THE INTERNET

Do your homework. Start searching for the best and most reliable Forex brokers and shortlist a few who are recommended and appear to be trustworthy. Then, do a small research. Focus on their website presentation, the validity of their registration, their online privacy policy and the legitimacy of their contact details.

In addition, explore the trading platforms they offer. This is among the best indicators of a broker's dependability. Offering dealing platforms such as Meta Trader or GTX ensures that the broker is registered which is definitely a good sign.

Other areas for comparison include the spread for each trade, the leverage plus the bonus amount they offer and the minimum balance necessary to open an account. Looking into these various features will assist you in analyzing a broker and eventually finding one best suited to your preferences.

DEMO ACCOUNT

The opportunity to trade in a demo account with virtual money is an important feature - one that can help you determine, whether the broker is a reliable one or not. Trading in a demo account permits you to learn the reigns of trading and that, while in the meantime using the features the broker offers such as the platform, spread and leverage.

DISCUSS IN THE FORUMS

One could easily find numerous Forex trading discussions in online forums where people share their thoughts, ask questions and discuss the marketplace. Forums such as these can assist in learning what other traders have discovered through experience. These discussions can provide an insight on all topics, from trading experiences to experiences with brokers. Prior to choosing a broker, one should discuss the various features offered with other experienced traders within these forums and therefore gauge the broker's reputation in the market.

WORK WITH HELPLINE

Do not hesitate to ask questions through the online chat service a brokerage offers. The service exists to help, so make sure you ask questions to alleviate any ambiguity attached with the trading process, platform, demo accounts, or any other issue you feel a broker should assist you with.

Clearly, there's a lot to think about when choosing a broker. However, by using these straightforward guidelines, you will be able to narrow down the list significantly. In the end, it more or less depends upon one's own needs and preferences. The past years due to the dramatic increase in forex traders more and more brokers also join the market and a large number of fraudsters also emerge alongside. The better one
researches, the greater the chances he or she will not only avoid a fraud but also make the best possible choice.

ACCOUNT TYPE

The decision of which type of account to open will most likely depend on the amount of capital you have to invest. Most brokerages offer two main account types: a "Mini" ($100-$200 minimum deposit) and a "standard" account ($1,000-$2,000 minimum deposit). Mini accounts are best suited to new or amateur traders looking to gain market experience and confidence with a smaller investment, and offer higher leverage, which you'll need in order to make money with such a small amount of initial capital. "Standard" account holders can expect to enjoy a wider variety of leverage options, but will have to invest a greater sum of money for the privilege. Although not as commonly advertised, many brokers provide a premium service for large investors (perhaps $100,000 - $250,000+), including additional VIP services, such as a dedicated fund manager and tailor made conditions.

Common to nearly all online brokers is the offer of a demo account, which allows users to get a feel for the software and gain trading experience without the risk of market exposure. Such simulations are undoubtedly beneficial to potential clients wishing to test the waters, but caveat emptor: they are not always representative of real-market, real-platform conditions, despite claims of full functionality. Do not be afraid to question a brokerage on this matter - an honest, reliable broker will admit the downfalls of a demo account.

SOFTWARE CONSIDERATIONS

The foreign currency market can move at a fast pace and will often require you to make quick decisions and executions, regardless of where you happen to be. Depending on your level and frequency of trading as well as travel habits, it may be wise to choose a brokerage that offers a web-based Java trading platform, which requires no download and enables you to trade from any location worldwide.

PAYMENT OPTIONS

Look for brokers that allow you to pay with credit card, as this is the easiest option by far and does not involve the necessity of transferring funds from online e-account. Other payment options typically offered include wire transfer, which is equally as secure as credit card, but expect to wait a number of days for it to clear and to have access to your funds.

SUPPORT

Perhaps one of the most crucial considerations and one that may potentially have a significant effect on your trading success is the issue of customer support. Whether you are a first time forex amateur or a FX vet, having the support and advice of a reliable, dedicated customer service team is undoubtedly invaluable, so it would prudent to do your homework on this one. The only way to gauge the quality of a support team is to contact them and see how they deal with your inquiries: are they fast, do they give reliable technical and market advice; do you get the sense that they know the industry well enough to advise others, or are they simply good sales people? This might not be so easy to find out, but as the only point of contact between yourself and the brokerage, it is important to do so. As with any business, pre-sale service might be more satisfactory than post-sale, so again, try to judge whether or not you are being helped or simply pitched.

PLATFORM, TOOLS & ANALYSIS

In the present online market place it is rare to find a company which does not offer real-time tools such as charting and price updates, but predictably the quality and availability of such applications will vary from broker to broker. Ideally you should have access to a wide range of tools, enabling you to assess the market 24 hours a day, making your trading decisions accordingly, and in addition your broker should also provide you with daily market reports, prepared in-house by professional analysts. These reports should cover the basics: economic news relevant to the major currencies, technical movements and general commentary. The better known, more reputable analysts have their reports published on a number of the larger online forex portals and forums, which is an indication that their data is considered accurate and reliable, which in turn tells you a little more about the reliability of the brokerage itself.

As previously mentioned, many trading platforms offer the same basic functions, but not all brokers cover all areas of the forex market, so before committing make sure your chosen platform will let you trade the currency pairs you require.

SPREADS

Spreads are an important factor to consider before investment and will certainly require some shopping around in order to find the best offer to suit your trading habits. The spread is the difference between the price at which currency can be bought and the price at which it can be sold at any given point in time. FX brokers don't charge "commissions", so this difference is how they make their money; therefore, the lower the spread, the lower the commission, and unlike stocks, currencies are not traded through a central exchange, so the spread may differ from broker to broker. Spreads differ according to account type, with mini accounts offering spreads between 1.5-2 times higher than those offered for Standard accounts, which in turn are higher than those offered to large volume traders with VIP status. "Fixed" spreads remain the same day or night, and despite market conditions, and although they are usually somewhat wider than the narrowest of variable spreads, they can be safer over the long term by providing a slightly higher level of predictability and a slightly lower level of risk. "Variable" spreads change according to market conditions (which may initially be attractive during a calm period, but once the market becomes busy, they are likely to widen considerably, meaning that the market will then have to move significantly in your favor before a profit is turned).

LEVERAGE

Unless you intend to invest a six-figure sum of capital, the use of leverage will be essential in order to make decent profits in forex. Generally speaking, the sum of money made during a successful trade amounts to just fractions of a single cent per unit, so if you are buying lots worth just a few thousand dollars or less, your profits will be minimal. This is where leverage comes into play: in effect by "borrowing" your broker's funds temporarily you will be able to make larger trades, which, if all goes according to plan, will lead to larger profits. Obviously, this practice involves an inherent risk: if the market takes a turn for the worse you risk losing a substantial sum of money, depending on the amount of leverage taken. For this reason it is advisable to do some further reading on leverage and margins prior to using leverage, so that you are fully informed before exposing yourself to the open market. Under normal market conditions, some common currency pairs are generally less volatile, and may warrant a higher level of risk taking, while more exotic currencies may not be predictable enough and traders would be advised to use less leverage when getting involved with such pairs. Mini accounts provide the highest levels of leverage, with some brokers offering up to x 400.

EDUCATION

While practicing on a demo account may help you improve somewhat and trading with real money might teach you some hard-learned lessons, the best way to improve your trading ability and provide yourself with a solid knowledge base is to educate yourself. To this effect, more and more online brokers are offering trading courses or tutorials, ranging from free five minute "introductions to forex" to curricula covering the smallest of details and costing thousands of dollars. Well established educational centers, such as the Online Trading Academy (OTA), with years of technical training experience are your best bet, providing solid instruction that will not only teach you the basics of the market, but also the technical side of the business (advanced technical analysis, charting, chart reading, Fibonacci calculations etc.). Some brokerages produce their own courses in conjunction with such trading centers, such as the course offered by Forexyard.com. Without educating oneself, the vast majority of built in market tools offered by trading platforms will be wasted on the amateur forex trader.

In summary, there are numerous factors to consider before choosing the right online forex broker, all of which should be researched to ensure that your trading account and broker will allow you to get the most from your investment. You must be aware that some brokers do not have your best interests at heart, but do not despair, as there are many reputable and reliable companies eager and capable of providing a professional service. As part of your research, be sure to visit the many online trader forums, where you can discuss any of the issues raised in this article with other traders, many of whom will already have been through the process of choosing a broker and will be able to advise you from their own experiences.

SCALPING FOREX BROKER

In order to take part in scalping the forex market, the first essential is a trading account with a Forex Broker. It is without a doubt, one of the most important decisions of your trading career. A great provider will smooth your way into the trading world, they will help you and guide you, they will be there when you are stuck, and let's face it - they will be there next year and not have absconded with your money! As I alluded in the previous sentence, there are many dodgy operators; you need to find the professionals. They need to have certain features for general trading, and they need yet more specific details for scalping.

So the first criteria, are they for real? This is quite simple, the test is not whether or not they have a professional website, not of course just believing hatever they say on that site. The best way to determine if this broker is a legitimate player is to check if they are registered with the appropriate local regulators. In the United States there are a number of bodies - one is the Financial Industry Regulatory Authority which you can find at finra.org. Other regulators are the Commodity Futures Trading Commission (CFTC) and the National Futures Association (NFA). Other countries have different authorities, for example in Australia it is ASIC (Australian Securities and Investments Commission). By choosing an unregulated broker you are risking your future trading funds, no joke.

There are many features to compare between forex brokers. Trading platforms vary from broker to broker, though you will find a fair number that actually utilize the same software package. Notably the Metatrader program is a popular choice especially among the smaller size providers. Look at the features they offer and compare things like the currency pair spreads, the method of dealing desk execution and any trading restrictions. The spread should of course be as small as possible, look for providers who can offer 2,3 or 4 pips at the most. You are ideally looking for a broker platform that has no dealing desk execution of orders to remove any conflict of interest (did you know many brokers will profit when you lose?). Make sure that trading restrictions (if any) do not hinder your ability to trade your system or method.

The next question to consider is what features are specifically important for scalping? The spread in this instance is especially important as quite often in a scalp trade, the target may only be as much as the spread itself! So of course the lowest spread as possible is what you want. The trading software platform must be super responsive and needless to say really, the data feed updating the system and it's charts must be absolutely real time. Always download and try demo trading from any broker you are considering and attempt to trade your method as if it were a live account. Accept no drawbacks in speed or accuracy in the programs as you can always look elsewhere.

If you are interested in utilizing automated trading robots for your accounts, you really should look into finding a broker that meets all the needs as expressed above and also offers the Metatrader 4 software package. Most of the commercially available trading robots run as plug-ins to this software and therefore require it to be installed so that they can run.

Always do your due diligence when choosing your broker. Use the internet, search engines are powerful and will easily find you plenty of reviews from fellow traders as to the quality and service you may expect from prospective providers.

QUESTIONS TO ASK WHEN CHOOSING ONLINE BROKERS

After studying the market and creating your own system, whether manual or one of those currency trading platforms, you feel that you are ready to get your feet wet. Naturally, you are looking only for the best forex brokers in the market to boost your position and expand your account. Choosing one, however, can be difficult especially since there's so many. Fortunately, you can short-list the names by asking the following questions.

WHAT IS THE LEVERAGE OF THE FIRM?

Leverage simply means the amount of money you are allowed to borrow from the firm when you open a position. This is subject to intensive monitoring by regulators to make sure nobody abuses this privilege. The numbers vary between online brokers though 1:50, 1:100 or 1:200. Generally, it's not advised to be beyond 200:1 and anybody who offers you that position is likely breaking the rules and you are going to be complicit in hiring the services. To better understand leverage, say you are trading $1,000... so with a leverage of 1:100 you are only required to pay $10. This is so you can expand your investments. Taken in another way, if your leverage is 1:100, your $1,000 investment just became $100,000. That means you gain profits or lose money quicker. You can trade as much as you want but when your account balance hits zero, the broker will then close all deals.

IS TECHNICAL AND CUSTOMER SUPPORT AVAILABLE 24/7?

You'll never know when you may need a helping hand. The best forex brokers, however, offer technical and customer support to better manage your funds. How can you access customer service, is it by phone, online chat or e-mail? Are the technical support staffs knowledgeable in the forex market? Understand that the capacity of the customer support service is reflective of the quality of the broker you are dealing with. In the same token, you should also ask what type of resources or trading tools that are being offered. Is the graphical user interface easy to use? Are there updated news-feeds or commentaries to keep you updated on current events? Is mobile trading available? You can't always be on your computer so tracking your account with your mobile device is essential.

IS THE BROKERAGE FIRM REGISTERED?

Major financial centres like the United States, United Kingdom, Australia, Hong Kong, Singapore, Japan and Finland are all regulated to make sure all the transactions are above board and nobody is manipulating the system to boost profits. Typically, the biggest stock broker in their respective areas is registered and required to submit reports to the oversight body. Another thing you should look at is the management composition of the brokerage firm such as its transaction history, experience and the types of accounts it is holding.

CHAPTER 7

IMPORTANT INFORMATION FOR US BASED TRADERS

A huge section of youngsters are joining the market as the trade volume crosses 4 trillion dollar mark everyday around the globe which about 53 times the trade volume of New York stock market. Just like every other field it is equally important for the Forex beginners to understand all the minute details of the market before entering it.

Each country has its own currency and all the international deals involve the changing of one currency into another which is called foreign exchange. The biggest financial market of the world is this foreign exchange markets, generally abbreviated as Forex.

There are lot of advantages like there is no middleman, so all the profit earned is not shared. An amount as low as 25$ can be invested in a deal though it is not suggested and the market remains open 24 hours so it is possible to trade as part time job because new comers are can open mini or micro accounts. A demo account is also a good option to practise before entering a real deal.

The basic nature of this market is that there is no central management so no one can control it. There is always an opportunity to gain money whether the market is moving up or down but not profitable when it is stagnant. One should try not to hold a sum with him for longer as it should be kept moving.

The 24 hour time duration is subdivided into four slots which are marked as Sydney, Tokyo, and London and New York session. Traders deal in their time slot but the best time is one in which two different sessions proceeds simultaneously.

Before entering FX, it is important to understand the concept of earning money. When the exchange rates of currency you possess are increased as compared to the rates at time you purchased it, profit can be earned by selling it. The exchange rate shows the ration of values of two currencies.

The exchange rates are represented as 'base currency/quote currency' which shows the units of quote currency required to buy one base currency. Traders use the terms long and short to symbolise the purchase and sale of money.

There is a fact that bid is always lower than ask. Bid is the value at which you can sell your base currency and ask is the amount at which you can purchase it. But before entering any deal you should learn to analyse market completely which can be done on three basis namely, sentimental, fundamental and technical analysis.

A balance between above three is most important when a forex beginner is process of framing his rules and disciplines which he is supposed to follow every time a deal is made. The success or failure depends on disciplines of the trader and how well one gain from his experience.

In this era where information can be an extremely powerful and strategic asset, whether to individuals or corporations, and information equals money, especially for a trader, shutting yourself off from news can be suicidal. The Forex market is extremely sensitive to the flow of news that is related to it, and major short-term currency moves are almost always preceded by changes in fundamental views influenced by the news. Traders around the world make a living by processing and translating information into money. Financial news services providers know how important news is to the Forex market players, and charge a premium for it. It is not uncommon to get hundreds of headlines of news that are potentially relevant to Forex trading from any news service provider on an average trading day.

Traders, especially those who day trade the Forex market, require the latest up-to-the-second news updates so as to facilitate their trading decisions which have to be made at lightning speed. They mostly make use of online financial newswire services such as Dow Jones Newswires, Bloomberg and Reuters, which display the latest financial news on their computer monitors. Since the speed of news dissemination is very important to traders, many opt for these online instant news services rather than depending on daily newspapers like the Wall Street Journal or the Financial Times which carry stale news that is of little use to traders.

The main reason why news is so important to Forex trading is that each new piece of information can potentially alter the trader's perceptions of the current
and/or future situation relating to the outlook of certain currency pairs. When people's opinions or beliefs are changed, they tend to act on these changed perceptions through buying or selling actions in the Forex market. Based on the news, these traders will be preparing to cover their existing positions or to initiate new positions.

A trader's action is based on the expectation that there will be a follow-through in prices when other traders see and interpret the same news in a similar way that he or she has, and adopt the same directional bias as the trader as a result.

News is a very important catalyst of short-term price movements because of the expected impact it has on other market players, and this is in a way an anticipatory reaction on the part of the trader as he or she assumes that other traders will be affected by the news as well.

If the news happens to be bullish, say for the US dollar, traders who react the fastest will be among the first to buy the US dollar, followed soon by other traders who may react slower to the news or are waiting for certain technical criteria to be met before jumping onto the bandwagon. And there will be those who join in the buying frenzy at a later stage when they get hold of the delayed news in the morning newspapers or from their brokers. This progressive entry of US dollar bulls over a period of time is what sustains the upward move of the US dollar against another currency, with the USD exchange rate going higher against other currencies. The reverse is true for bearish news, traders will sell because they know that others will soon be selling, thus pushing the USD exchange rate down. This is based on the assumption that since other traders will be getting the same pieces of news, they will be also tend to be affected the same way.

Publicly released news is disseminated to the various newswires. Any trader with access to these wires can tap into the information given out, and react accordingly in the Forex market. However, institutional players do get information that retail traders don't, as they get privy access to order book information in their computer systems, and may also know something that others don't through their personal contacts in the industry.

In the world of Forex trading, there are no rules or restrictions against insider trading! Anyone who possesses information that is known only to a select few can and do trade that information in the Forex market.

Sometimes, such news may give an unfair advantage to these institutional players, but at other times, this isolated news access may not translate into real market action if other players do not have that information.

Think of it this way: The Forex market is dependent on news, for if there is no news, there would be little or negligible price movements in the market. Even if currencies may move according to the technicals sometimes, the technicals have been established previously by news or expectations of future news, and so the influence of news on currency prices is inevitable and inescapable.

CHAPTER 8

UNDERSTANDING FOREX PIPS VALUE

Pips and 'pips values' represent one of the most misunderstood concepts in Forex trading. Newbies, especially, often have trouble grasping the idea behind pips -- but, a solid understanding of pips is crucial to successful Forex investing.

If you have had trouble with pips, then today may be your lucky day. I'm going to attempt to clarify things once and for all with a brief pips tutorial.

Hopefully you are already familiar with the concept of 'basis points'. One basis point is equal to one one-hundredth of one percent, and represents the smallest increment of change measured for any financial instrument.

Take interest rates as an example. If the interest rate on your credit card rises from 10.12 percent to 10.13 percent, then it has risen by 1 basis point.

Pips are the Forex markets version of basis points. Let's say that the exchange rate for the EUR/USD pair move from 1.4465 to 1.4468. This movement represents a shift of 3 Pips, and may be good or bad depending on which currency you are holding.

Here's the catch, though. Notice that the shift took place on the 4th decimal, which is the ten-thousandths place, or 1/10,000 of a percentage point? You have a shift of one ten-thousandth instead of one one-hundredth.

The reason for this is that most currencies (with the exception of the Yen) are quoted out to four decimal places. This means you get to take advantage of even the most minute shifts as you trade on high volume.

In order to calculate Pips for the common, four decimal currency pairs, you must divide the value of 1 Pip by the exchange rate:

$$1 \text{ Pip} = 1/10000\text{th} / \text{exchange rate}$$

Now, what happens when you are dealing with the Japanese Yen? In this currency pair, we find an exception to the rule because the Yen is quote out only to the hundreds place, or 1/100.

For the USD/JPY pair (or vice versus), your formula would be:

$$1 \text{ Pip} = 1/100\text{th} / \text{exchange rate}$$

Now that you know how to calculate Pips for any currency pair, you must look at what an actual Pip is worth to you in real dollar terms. This value is known as "pips value". In order to do this, we must bring 'lot size' into the equation.
If you purchase a standard lot of 100,000 pairs of EUR/USD at 1.4465. , your formula will be as follows:

$$\text{Pip Value} = (0.0001 / 1.4465) \times 100{,}000 = 6.91$$

So, a pip at this exchange rate is worth 6.91 Euro. Do not look for exact numbers here. What you need to pay attention to is the fact that '6.91' represents the average gain or loss per change in pips.

In other words, a fluctuation of 2 pip from 1.4465 to 1.4467 isn't going to raise your profit or loss by a full Euro or more. Try doing the calculation for a 2 pip rise, and you'll see that your pips value goes up only to 6.192.

I recommend getting comfortable with these basic calculations first, and then moving on to the calculations of actual profit and loss, which will require you to factor in bid price and ask price.

Also, remember that your online broker usually calculates pip and pips values for you, and you do not have to know how to do the math. It's just good business to be able to do it yourself.

Pip in Forex Trading - The Final Hit In general terminology the abbreviation "pip" may refer to many things like Protective Industrial Products, Picture-in-Picture, Personal Identity Provider, Partners in Protection, Preferred Internet Provider, Performance Index Paper etc.

In currency trading "pip" stands for "percentage in point". This is the smallest increment of change in forex trade. It is the smallest number in quotation of a currency.

In foreign exchange market, rates are quoted to the fourth decimal point. For example, if the price of a burger in the market is $1.22, in forex market the same burger will be quoted as 1.2200. Under this example, the 4th decimal point will constitute one pip and normally equals 1/100th of 1%.

The above is the general rule. Exception to this is the quotation in USD/JPY which is only up to 2 decimal points. This is because Japanese Yen has not been revalued since Second World War. Thus in case of Yen, the quotation is only up to 1/100th of yen as against 1/1000th with other major currencies.

All other currencies in relation to Yen will be quoted up to 2 decimal points. The usual pairs will be AUDJPY, CADJPY, CHFJPY, EURJPY, GBPJPY etc.

Other factors that go in the understanding of a pip are trading size, extent of leverage and rate of a currency pair. In case of USD, with a leverage of 1:100 and trading volume of one lot, one pip will have a value of $10.
The above will be the minimum incremental value by which USD will fluctuate. Thus, if there is a one pip change, that means one has gained or lost $10.

One pip value for one lot in USD will be equivalent to $10 in case of all currency pairs not involving JPY. Where JPY is the other currency in a pair, one point value will be equivalent to $1000 / USDJPY rate.

Closely associated with pips is the "spread". This is the difference between bid price at which a forex broker is willing to buy the first currency of a pair and the offer or sell price at which he is willing to sell the first currency of a   pair. The difference between bid and ask prices is the spread.

If EUR/USD is quoted as 1.4205/1.4207, the spread will be equivalent to EUR 0.0002 or 2 pips. The size of a spread depends upon the popularity of a currency pair. The more popular a pair, smaller the spread and vice versa.

Pip spread may be better for major players which trade in large quantities as compared to retail or individual traders. Spot prices on EUR/USD are usually no more than 3 pips wide (0.0003). With increased competition, pip spreads have shrunk on major pairs to as little as 1 to 2 pips.

CALCULATING PIP VALUE DEMYSTIFIED

Knowing to what extent the price change is going to affect your position and account is essential for a trader. For that you have to calculate the value of one pip of price movement. There are lots of examples on the 'net, and some of them look rather confusing. While in fact calculating pip value is very easy to do.

First of all you should know by now that the currency specified first in exchange rates is base currency, and the one in the second position is called terms currency. You always buy or sell the base currency. And the value of pip you will get is in terms currency. Multiply how much you buy or sell with a pip size: say for 6 mini-lots of NZDUSD pip value is 6'000NZD * 0.0001 = 6USD/pip; or for 2 full lots of USDJPY it is 200'000USD * 0.01 = 2'000JPY/pip.

Sometimes you are fine with what you get in a previous step. Specifically, this is the case when terms currency of your trade is what you want to see. For example, you trade NZDUSD and want to get pip value in dollars, then you got 6USD per pip already and don't need to go any further.

But you may want to see this value expressed in a currency other than the terms currency. Say you want to now how your account would be affected by 1 pip price movement and you made a deposit in pounds. In this case you'll have to take exchange rate of the pair including GBP (or other currency you are interested in) and the terms currency of your trade (USD for NZDUSD, or JPY for USDJPY). Say rates are 1.6977GBPUSD and 161.50GBPJPY.

Next step is to look if our currency (i.e. GBP) is base or terms currency in these rates. If it is base currency we divide the above result (i.e. pip value expressed in terms currency) with the rate: 6USD/1.6977GBPUSD = 3.53GBP or 2000JPY/161.50GBPJPY = 12.38GBP.

If it is terms currency though, we multiply the above result with the rate. Say our account denominated in swiss francs (instead of pounds). USDCHF rate is 1.0624, CHFJPY is 89.61. Then 1 pip value of the two trades above will be expressed in francs as: 6USD * 1.0624 USDCHF = 6.37CHF (CHF is terms currency here), but 2000JPY / 89.61 CHFJPY = 22.32CHF (CHF is base currency in this pair).

In case the last two examples still leave you wondering, try to look at them in the following way. 89.61CHFJPY means we pay 89.61 units of terms currency (JPY) for 1 unit of base currency (CHF). That is 89.61 JPY per CHF, or mathematically speaking 89.61 JPY/CHF. (Yes, the actual meaning of exchange rates is exactly opposite to the order we see in forex symbols; it is even more confusing since sometimes symbols include slash, like CHF/JPY). Now if you substitute this mathematical meaning into formula from the last paragraph, you'll notice that one of the currency symbols within the fraction will get reduced and another one will end up in the numerator position: 2000 * JPY / 89.61 * JPY / CHF = (2000 / 89.61) * CHF = 22.32CHF. Thus you've got exactly what it says - 22.32 swiss francs (per pip of 2 full lots of USDJPY).

How to Calculate Forex Pip Value

We're all used to dollars and cents (as you're used to the currency in your country), but when you enter the Forex market, you need to learn a new term: Pip. What does it mean and how do you calculate a Forex pip value?

Pip

The pip is defined as the smallest increment a currency pair can take. For instance, for the USD/CAD pair, a pip is 0.0001. For the USD/JPY pair a pip is 0.01. A pip is also known as a point.

Recently, many Forex brokers changed their price quotes from a 4 digit quote to a 5 digits one. This practically changed the smallest increment a currency pair can move, but the pips have remained the same.

There used to be a trick that you could use with 5 digits quote to know what a pip is, but it doesn't work every time anymore:
The trick is simple: take the exchange rate and count 5 digits backwards. For instance, today, the USD/CAD is at 1.04328 (a 5 digit quote). Count 5 digits from the first: 1, 0, 4, 3, 2. The 2 is the 5th digit in the qquote and it's at the 4th position after the decimal point, so a pip for the USD/CAD is 0.0001. This is also true for the EUR/GBP, EUR/USD and a lot of other currency pairs.

For the USD/JPY it's a different story. The USD/JPY exchange rate was historically over 100 Yen for a Dollar. This is why the Pip value for the USD/JPY is 0.01.

However, the USD has lost value in relation to the Yen, so it's value today stands at 86.693. Even so, a pip is still 0.01, because this used to be the place of the 5th currency in the quote. This is also true for the CHF/JPY and other currencies involving the Yen.

Another way to know is to simply find out if your broker is running 4 digit quotes (in which case the pip is at the last digit) or 5 digit quotes (in which case the pip is at the position before last).

How to calculate the value of a pip

A pip is always calculated by the base currency (the second one in the pair). This is multiplied by the lot size with which you're trading. For the standard lot which has 100,000 units, the pip value for the USD/CAD is 10 CAD or $9.59 (by today's exchange rate of 1.04328 USD/CAD). This is the calculation: 10 CAD /1.04328 = $9.59.

For the EUR/USD the value of a pip is $10 which is pretty simple. For all standard lots when the USD is the base currency a pip is $10.

For a mini lot with only 10,000 units, the Pip will be 10 times less, or just $1 for the EUR/USD and $0.959 for the USD/CAD.

It's important to be able calculate the value of a Forex pip. After all, this is the most basic term in the Forex trading world.

Forex Trading Pips For Peeps

When forex trading, pips are vital for day trading. So what are they? Price Interest Points or better known as pips are often encountered around day trading currencies. This is the representation of which the price of a particular currency is interpreted on its smallest fluctuation.

There are two kinds of forex trading pips; one is the static pip value and the other is the variable pip value. The static pip value is where other mayor currencies not including the US Dollar is being traded as the base currency. And the value is constant as relative to the Dollar. As per the variable pip value is where the US Dollar is the mayor currency or is the quote currency in the dominant base currency traded. For both pips, the key is always the most current exchange rate.

To be able to determine the forex trading pips, one must have to be able to compute the value based on the current exchange rate for the particular currency. The value of the pip entirely depends on the amount of the trade lot or contract. The most common size of a contract sold by forex brokers is about one hundred thousand units. In a static value pip, 1 pip would be equal to 0.0001 of the currency traded for which is the US Dollar.

To be able to get its value, one must first be able to determine the exchange rate of the mayor currency against the US Dollar then multiplied by the currency quoted by the fourth decimal place. On the other hand, the variable pip value one pip unit is equivalent to 1000 and is divided against the value of the exchange rate of the currency being traded for.

CHAPTER 9

THE RISKS IN FOREX TRADING

In the last few years, Forex trading has quickly become one of the most popular home businesses. People are intrigued as to how simple it can be to increase their income while at the comfort of their own home. But in addition to the possible gain, they also realize how quickly that income can disappear if they are not properly educated and are not making smart trading decisions.

Even with all the convenient features that forex trading offers, the average person will still hesitate in investing because of the risk. Before getting into any trading, you should anyways make sure you do some research on the topic. Get as much info as possible to make sure you are completely comfortable investing your hard earned money.

very decision you make in life will always have a risk involved. Accepting a new job, taking that flight on your vacation, and even driving to work in the morning, can be a risk. Some of these are risks we can not avoid. Yet some of them are risks we can avoid, if we chose to. It's impossible to eliminate all risks, but you do have the ability to minimize the effect the risk can have.

Now try to imagine Forex as an aspect in your life. You can definitely avoid it if you chose to, or you can take a risk.

Let's take driving to work for an example. Would you drive yourself to work if you didn't know how to drive? Didn't have a license? Of course you wouldn't! You would be making a HUGE risk that could result in a major negative outcome.

Now let's take the Forex trade market. You would never just invest your life savings and hope for the best would you? No, of course not. You're much smarter then that!

Forex trading has the ability to bring in a profit of 100 times your initial investment. But if not trading wisely, it has the possibility to lose most, or in other cases, all of your investment.

You should always being trading with an amount of money you can afford to lose. Once you have become more familiar with the system, and you are making a constant profit, you can begin to invest more.

There are dozens of sites available to educate you on Forex and everything you need to know about trading. A smart investor is always a profitable investor!

Take the time to educate yourself with all the forex terms and trading methods. Learn the ins and outs of the trade so you can make wise decisions and pave your way to financial freedom.

The Forex trade is a non-centralized market. This means that there is no standard in the foreign exchange price. If you are planning to invest you own money, you will need a broker to make the actual transactions.

Choosing a good dealer is very important, and completing a background check on them is essential. You want to make sure that you agree to their terms and you fully understand what they are performing for you. You can visit the local Customer Protection Bureau and the Better Business Bureau to find out information on the broker you choose.

To minimize the risks in Forex trading, you need to know the best time to enter and exit the market. This will become your basic strategy on forex trading. Once you have spent time learning about the trade, you will be able to read the financial chart and be able to analyze the market accurately.

There is also, what they call, automated forex trading programs. These downloadable software programs can be an essential tool when trading forex. This software has the ability to make the right trade for you, and in addition provides market analysis which will help you monetize market trends.

There are several of these programs on the market and most can provide you with all the help you need to make profitable forex trading decisions. I would suggest that you take a peak at some of the offers out there and feel them out for yourself. Most come with a 60 day money back guarantee, so for once in your life, there will be no risk!

Here are a few valuable tips about the risks involved in trading in the Forex Market, that may be of help to you.

You could lose your investment.

This sounds too obvious to mention, but it's true. There is no guarantee of success. Between the time you place a trade and the time you close your trade, there is much that can still take place. For one thing, fluctuations in the foreign exchange rate will affect your potential profit, the price of your contract, and your potential losses in the deal.

Good management of your accounts is essential. However, be aware always that you could lose your entire investment. Prices can move in a direction that does not favor your position. High leverage can result in losses in excess of your initial deposit. It's also possible that, depending on your agreement with your dealer, you may also end up paying for more losses.

Be wary of anyone stating that your investment is protected. In reality, forex trades are not guaranteed by any organization, nor are your deposits to trade forex contracts insured. If a dealer goes bankrupt, the funds deposited by that dealer in an FDIC-insured bank account may not be protected.

The Internet has its own risks

There is always a possibility, however remote, that an online system failure may occur. This would put you in a very difficult position, keeping you from making new orders, making changes to or canceling existing orders. In light of this risk, it's best to obtain the contact information, such as the telephone numbers and addresses of the companies and individuals you are dealing with online, so you may continue your business with as little disruption as possible.

Any investment carries the risk of fraud, and you should protect yourself against this as well. Scams are prevalent and increasing in number throughout the Internet. Due diligence on your part is definitely in order before you begin, and during trading.

Avoid deals that sound too good

Understand and remember that risk is inherent in forex trading, and anyone who assures you of the opposite is to be avoided.

Opportunities that sound too good to be true are worthy of extra caution from you. In fact, it may be best just to stay away from them altogether. Get-rich-quick schemes definitely fall into this category, and often tend to be fraudulent.

Before you do business with anyone, be sure you know as much about them as you can, and be satisfied that they are reputable and trustworthy. If you cannot be certain that they are completely legitimate, it is best to not do business with that company or individual. One place to do your background check is at the National Futures Association (NFA). Visit the Background Affiliation Status Information Center, or BASIC, available through NFA's web site, where you can find registration and disciplinary records about forex companies' and individuals in the futures industry. Not all brokers are required to register with NFA, but this is a good place to start your search for pertinent information.

Before you make any trading decisions, consult with your financial advisor, get excellent forex training through a reputable program. If you are new to forex, open a free demo account to learn how to trade online. if you have some experience, start trading now with an active account. Even with the inherent risks of currency trading, you can gain confidence from experience, and join the thousands of people worldwide who are making good money every day.

BENEFITS VS RISK OF FOREX TRADING

Forex trading is not suitable to all investors. It is important that you understand the benefits as well as the risk of trading before mastering in any field of investment. Remember, you can build wealth in forex, but you can destroy it as well. By minimizing the risk, you should basically understand forex trading program.

LIQUIDITY

Forex market is so unique that it is extremely liquid in the market, especially for the most popular currency pairs. There are up to 1.8 trillion US dollar being traded everyday. The trading volume is even 50 X larger than New York Stock Exchange. Participants are rapidly growing, from interbank to commercial company, non-financial company, private speculators and so forth. Unlike stocks marketing, there are always sellers and buyers on the other side. Due to its liquidity, you can
stop/ limit/ open or close position freely. They always have some reason to trade in Forex.

For instance, Malaysia borrow money from Japan to build a   D1, the process take 5 years, they hedge a rate first so that the fluctuating currency rate won't affect the repayment.... Hence, the price will be more stable and not fluctuating as stock market. None of a trader could affect trend of currency.

24/7 Market

There are always buyers and sellers trading currencies in day and night. It allows you to respond even though some investment markets are closed. This minimizes the "overnight gap" risk. Normal operation starts from Sunday 5pm until Friday 4 pm at EST.

LOW STARTING EQUITY REQUIREMENT

For day trading stocks is not an affordable investment for most people, especially those employees who earn secure income monthly. It requires the minimum of $25,000 to open a day trading account. You may doesn't need to, if you gain satisfying profit and take it out within 3 days.

On the contrary, for Forex accounts, I have seen starting equity requirements as low as $200. We can manage forex account by credit cards. It is so easy to open an account, without much cash barrier. But ...think deeper! This carries risk as well as benefits to you. What do you think?

Since the starting equity can be very low, it highly encourages more people to participate in low entry level. It gives opportunity to the investor who is low to set up "educational account " and learn trading in minimum equity. It is a method to sharpen our skills and strategies. They can be trained to utilize strategies to set appropriate stop/limit to maximize profit.

However, it brings lesson to those who are lack of experience or financial illiteracy to take the speculative risk. It also lures people who dare to take risk without proper strategies or tools. This reckless manner of investment makes no difference with gamble. They might lose. At last, their cash will easily flowing out but can hardly understand a lesson.

If you are one of them, I suggest that you can train yourself by applying secret forex strategies by forex demo trading, or attending forex courses before you fight for your profit. See how quickly you can make or lose on trades in the real environment, but without risking your own money. It's very important to have strategies, so that you become financial literacy. Please be the one who control your trading situation, do not being fooled by the market.

Leverage up to 400:1

You may call it margin trading. In Forex trading market, you can execute trading up to 400X of initial margin/cost. which means I can execute trade of $400 by just $1 of initial margin. A high leverage gives chance to those who build in small capital, to have huge potential. Although the profit potential is high, remember, the loss potential is equally great.

There are 10: 1, 20:1, and up to 400:1 of leverage. Most Forex brokers do this on sliding scale. The smallest account will can get the privilege of higher leverage. Example: US$200 initial margin can control up to $200,000 margin(leverage 400:1); A larger US$20,000 initial margin will be advised to control of $400,000 (leverage 20:1). It is important to aware of the size of risk rather than your starting cost. Once your account increases, your margin will drop to 400:1 then 200:1 to 20:1. However, the choices of leverage are all depends on investors' appetite for risk.

Because of the generous margin provision, it attracts small investors. You must carefully consider your monetary objectives, level of experience and appetite to risk before deciding the leverage. Professional forex
traders rarely use more than 10:1. In their opinion, high leverage speeds up high level risk of margin call.

COMMISSION FREE AND LOW TRANSACTION COST

Transaction cost carries much difference between stocks and forex trading. It is much more cost efficient to invest in the Forex market, in terms of both commissions and transaction fees. Stock commissions charge you correlated with the level of service offered by broker. It ranges from a low of $7.95-$29.95 per trade with on-line forex brokers to over $100 per trade with traditional brokers. For instance, for $7.95, customers receive no access to market information, research or other relevant data. At the high end, traditional brokers offer full access to research, analyst stock recommendations, etc. In contrast, on-line Forex brokers charge significantly lower transaction and commission free. All stop, limit, entry and exit orders are commission free. Investors only need to pay spread between ask/bid price. In general, the width of the spread in a FX transaction is less than 1/10 as wide as a stock transaction, which typically includes a 1/8 wide bid/ask spread. For example, if a broker will buy a stock at $22 and sell at $22.125, the spread equals .006. For a FX trade with a 5 pip wide spread, where the dealer is willing to buy EUR/USD at .9030 and sell at .9035, the spread equals .0005.

BI-DIRECTIONAL AND FLEXIBLE TRADING

Investors able to gain profit in bullish or bearish, buy or sell condition. Even during ecomomy recession, it's possible to make money in Forex. There are many trends of currencies that you can choose to have long term or short term, aggressive or conservative types of investment, based on your objectives and need, by appropriate strategies.

ONLINE FOREX TRADING

By trade online, you can know the up-to-date account information, mentor analysis, news and report. Continuous connection to market allows us to monitor risk and profit at real time. We clearly know our interest on daily.

COMPOUND PROFITS

Similar as Fixed deposit, the profit earned will be accumulated automatically to account and reinvest for greater returns. This allows investors to have maximum profit without adding risk.

FREE ONLINE EDUCATION

Free news, free charts, free mentor and consultant, demo trading, strategy tips other reference guides are easily obtained. Myriad of online education provides knowledge and latest trend of Forex, guide you to the tips master Forex.

FURTHER REDUCTION OF RISKS IN FOREX TRADING

Forex trading is conceivably a great financial instrument towards financial freedom depending on how we turn this instrument into our excellent financial assistant.

Great number of information about Forex trading has been posted in the internet for our reviewing. These sites detail out the advantages as well as the disadvantages of trading Forex. A beginner who browses through all these sites gets confuse easily and eventually end up with the assumption that trading Forex is of high risks and not worth venturing in. True, trading Forex has its risks but then which financial instrument that generates high returns is without risks?

The question here should be how can the risks be reduced in order to utilize Forex trading as a tool to financial freedom? This is another issue that is widely available in the websites. The obvious one is to appoint a good coach to guide us through the proven strategies in determining the market movement and subsequently the entry and exit point of a trade. Not only that, the coach should also help in recommending regulated and trustworthy brokers.

Aside from those that the coaches offer, what is it that we ourselves can do to lower the risk even further? The tips below are not particularly innovative but are often overlooked. For that reason, we should constantly remind ourselves on the three tips below while trading Forex.

Do not deviate from the strategy taught as these strategies are usually backed with established track record. It is acceptable to experiment or challenge a strategy but do so using a demo account. Any trading carried out should not be base on feelings. What are the winning probabilities for every trade executed through feelings? How many times will Lady Luck side us?

Beginners have to work hard on practicing the strategies. Regular and frequent practicing allows us to comprehend the strategies and also to discover our style of trading. Regular practicing may sounds simple but not easy to follow especially for those who are bogged down with busy daily schedule. In this case, priorities have to be reset and rearranged.

For anything that is dynamic, random events are bound to happen. So is Forex. It is a dynamic market and hence randomness does arise. The term randomness by itself is self explain and therefore the market movement at this time could not be anticipated. No strategy so far can capture this randomness, which is why there should not be a strategy claiming 100% winning trades. For beginners that experienced a couple of losing trades in succession should not be too concern. Stay with the strategies. However if your confidence runs low, contact your coach for further guidance. Good and reliable coaches do provide follow up sessions to ensure that beginners comprehend the fundamental of the strategies.

WAYS TO REDUCE THE RISKS OF FOREX TRADING

Before you get into the forex game, you really need to look at some forex review system trading information first. Remember that the business of forex trading is something that can put you at great risk. You can stand to make a lot of money but at the same time you can also lose all that money if you are not careful. So what do you need to do?

Pick a platform and your brokers - This is something that you need to do with a lot of care because you are going to be placing your trust in these people and the platform. One way to do this is to go through forex review system trading information that you can get from books, magazines and even online sites.

Look for corporate profiles and investment portfolios - Other information you need includes the right profiles when it comes to the corporations that you want to do business with in forex trading. Forex review system trading information is important when you are looking for material on the matter. Through reviews, you will be able to gain access on actual assessments on small investors and even get evaluations from some of the top financial groups that you may have heard of. The comparisons will be helpful for you to make wise decisions because what you need to find is the key information on the market.

Get technical analysis - Now you may be wondering why you really need forex review system trading information. The fact is that if you are getting into the industry, you will need to get a clear picture of certain brokers' performances over a certain length of time. You can look at their records over a specific period or you can also get a technical analysis of the specific currencies that they have dealt in. Veterans in the industry usually do these reviews. That means that they are also people who have done their own trades successfully. The data that they provide can be somewhat very accurate and useful. It will mostly likely be written in a clear language so that you can understand what is really going on in the forex industry.

Compare and contrast - If you really don't know which corporate portfolio to choose and which brokers to deal with, you can make a good comparative analysis by using forex review system trading information. This way, you will find the best people willing to handle the investment that you make and they will also listen to the way that you want that investment to be controlled as well. In the end, you will still be taking risks but at least your risks will be minimal.

CHAPTER 10

NEWS AND FUNDAMENTAL ANALYSIS

The name of the game in Forex trading is predicting the movements of the market. Whoever can answer the question "What will the EUR/USD do next?" is sure to make a nice bundle. The only way to really do this with accuracy is via Forex fundamental analysis A.K.A Forex news.

Putting aside the age old dilemma about Forex fundamental analysis vs technical analysis, no one debates the importance of watching Forex news and adjusting your trading accordingly.

At the end of the day, Forex news and Forex fundamental analysis is what drives the market. A war in one country or a political revolution in another is the kind of news that will have a direct impact on the Forex market and its future trends.

No one is saying that you should ignore technical analysis, the Forex charts will definitely help you in your trading but news and fundamental analysis are two tools you should focus your attention on when trading this market.
Most Forex brokers offer trading platforms with integrated news and Forex fundamental analysis, and if your broker does not, it might be time to move on.

The worst mistake a Forex trader can make is to trade Forex in an abyss. Forex is not a casino and if you do not have a technique including news and fundamental analysis, then you are making a fundamental mistake that will cost you big losses.

In addition, some might find reading the charts to be a little too technical and complex for them, but it is safe to say that anyone trading Forex can handle the task of reading the Forex news and fundamental analysis, They are usually written in simple language that is easy to understand and digest. What you do with the information you get in today's news is another story completely.

Forex fundamental analysts can take one look at today's news and conclude that the USD will rise or fall today against the Yen, something that requires training over an extended period of time. Having said that, a large part of fundamental analysis or analyzing the Forex news, is common sense that any person with no prior training can do, at least on a basic level.

Forex Fundamental Analysis - Do You Need to Know These?

One of the ways to plan a trading strategy on Metatrader or any other platform is through fundamental analysis. This approach involves exploring the market as well seemingly unrelated news and events, such as:

a) Political events almost always influence the market as well as national security related incidents that have a power to bring down or boost up a currency. For example, the oil rig explosion in the Gulf of Mexico gave a boost to the oil prices.
b) Indices - GDP, CPI, PPI, BOP, PMI. All of them influence the quote of the national currency. If the US GDP, for example, is lower than expected the dollar will start losing to other currencies.
c) Financial data - stock prices, interest rates, bonds and such. In times of an economic crisis, central banks might leave the interest rate unchanged if the economic recovery or growth is insufficient or if the country did recovered from the crisis, the

purpose is to avoid big interest-rate gaps between other countries.

For example, the interest rate serves as a base for the exchange rate of the national currency. If the interest rate is raised, the exchange rate of the currency also rises due to increased demand. That's why trader that uses fundamental analysis to generate signals or confirm trends should follow central bank announcements of the interest rate.

Fundamental analysis also includes the aspect of traders' and analysts' expectations of an index performance. For example, just before the Weekly Inventory Report released in the US, the oil trading prices usually go up and after the release they act according to the results. Positive business and political news can result in increased investments in the national currency (because traders are huge fans of stability).

One of the best trading platforms that provide the trader with every tool needed for successful work is Metatrader. It's a comprehensive platform (forex, oil, CFD, commodities, silver, gold, metals) that has instruments for both technical and fundamental analysis.

Comprehending fundamental analysis

Before looking at the different types of forex fundamental analysis, it is important to first of all understand the basics. In forex trading, fundamental analysis can be described as a form of market study that entails examining the current, past and future economic status of countries so as to trade in foreign currencies more efficiently. It provides informative data on how political and economic situations affect the performance of currencies in the marketplace. Normally the numbers and statements provided in speeches by pivotal political figures as well as economists are referred to as economical declarations amongst traders in the forex marketplace. These statements usually have a huge influence on foreign currencies movements in the market. Of particular interest, a proclamation that relates to the economic status of the United States of America is usually of uttermost importance.

Discussed herein are the different types of forex fundamental analysis that you need to be aware of as a forex trader.

THE ECONOMIC CALENDAR

The first fundamental analysis that you ought to be aware of when trading in foreign currencies is the economic calendar. This is specially developed by economist so as to be in a position to foretell various economic numbers as well as values in regards to the past months. It holds the next data. For instance, if the current forecast is much better than the past numbers, then the US dollar is expected to be stronger than the other currencies.

However, when the news are expected traders normally confirm with the actual data. If you study the oil prices, an increase in price will end up in declining of currencies for countries that greatly rely on huge amounts of oil importations, i.e. USA, Japan and UK amongst others.

SPEECHES BY PROMINENT POLITICAL AND ECONOMIST FIGURES

The second fundamental analysis are political and economist statements. Politics plays a huge role in the performance of the forex market. As such it is normally important as a trader. For example in the United States of America, speeches by certain political and economist figures are usually closely observed by forex traders asnthe declarations they make usually influences outcomes in the market place greatly. These may range from the chairperson of the federal reserve bank of America or the treasury secretary. Given that success in this market is purely speculative, it is vital that as a trader you pay close attention to these statements as they may play a role in determining the type of foreign currency you would wish to engage in.

NUMERIC THAT INFLUENCE THE FOREX MARKET

Last but not least, forex fundamental analysis entails knowing what figures actually influence the forex market place. These are: - Interest rate: Conventionally, whenever a country increases its interest rates, the local currency normally increases in strength since investors are bound to move their assets to such countries with an aim of gaining high returns. - Employment Rate: Normally when there is a high turn over in a country, it acts as an indicator of reduced economic activities. As a result, the interest rates decreases which results in poor performance of the local currency.

Other figures to watch out for in forex fundamental analysis are trade balance, gross domestic product (GDP) as well as budget.

Use Fundamental Analysis and Technical Analysis to in Trades

There are two types of analysis used in the Forex market - technical analysis and fundamental analysis. Both types of analysis will result in different charting predictions. Many traders tend to stick with just one type of analysis and may win a decent number of trades. However, by understanding how both types of analysis interact, you significantly increase your winning trade percentage.

Fundamental analysis deals with the economic, political and social data that influences the strength of a currency while technical analysis deals specifically with currency price movements. Technical traders rely on charting trends to predict future currency price movements while fundamental traders make their decisions based on news reports released by governments etc.

Both styles of trading can be effective, although to maximize trading opportunities, a successful Forex trader needs to understand both Forex charting trends and how news reports can influence currency movement away from trends. It sounds complex and many traders opt to stick with one style of trading... maybe it is why 95% of Forex traders lose money, or maybe that is a coincidence.

For example, if you rely solely on technical analysis and your favorite trading indicator has identified the start of a basic trend, you are convinced this is a great trading opportunity and quickly enter into a trade. However, shortly after placing your trade there is a sudden 40 pip drop and you hit your stop-loss figure. You are scratching your head and puzzled why it took the sudden downturn.

If you had been monitoring the Forex news reports due out that day you would have fully understood as it just happened to announce interest rates had been lowered. You would have lost a substantial amount of money by ignoring fundamental analysis and been guilty of relying too heavily in technical analysis.

The moral of the story is to fully understand Forex charting; you need to examine both fundamental analysis and technical analysis. It is even more crucial that you understand which types of fundamental analysis will impact on currency pairs you are trading if you rely on automated Forex trading robots as they are predominantly configured to identify trends through technical analysis.

Automated Forex trading robots can serve a very useful purpose if you use them wisely and know when you should manually take control. There are certainly plenty of trading robots available nowadays and I am currently evaluating some of them to see whether they can complement my preferred trading style.

With the ever increasing popularity of online forex trading worldwide, more and more people have been trying their hand at the currency markets. The strategies employed by the new along with experienced trader come sometimes differ greatly.

Fortunately, all forex traders belong to one of three main groups. They are either technical traders, fundamental traders or they are traders that utilize techniques from both disciplines. Lets take a closer look at the three.

FUNDAMENTAL TRADING

Fundamental traders utilize macro and micro economics to predict the general direction or shift in a trend. Their analysis involves the current economic situation of the currency issuer as well as economic events that may affect the specific country and currency.

Since a wide variety of events can affect any one currency, fundamental traders usually have their eyes on the news. Anything from political upheaval to natural disasters can have a huge effect on the economic situation. The key is how they react to this information with their given understanding of global economics. They must be ready to react to changes on the fly.

Fundamental analysis is used for both long term and short term trades. Major economic news releases such as unemployment rates, trade balance announcements and interest rate changes are usually of great interest and can offer great insight to the future trend of a currency pair. Fundamental traders generally put more faith in fundamental analysis than they do technical analysis. As such, there are some that concentrate on economics alone.

Unfortunately, a true understanding on the workings of global economics is difficult to attain. For the rest of us, there is Technical forex trading.

TECHNICAL TRADING

Technical trading is by far the most popular and well known strategy employed in the forex market today. The reason is simple. Technical analysis is far easier to grasp than fundamental analysis is for the vast majority of traders out there. Technical analysis is also far easier (as well as a lot quicker) to teach, which is why most forex trading courses out there concentrate on the technical aspects of trading. Technical analysis enjoys widespread recognition as a result.

Technical analysis attempts to predict the future movement of the market from past market movements. It is based on the assumption that history eventually repeats itself. The information seen on the charts are viewed as "complete" as it is assumed that the price accurately reflects the supply, demand and external factors such as the political and economic situation for agiven currency. It is also the heavy study of market trends.

TECHNICAL AND FUNDAMENTAL ANALYSIS COMBINED

Finally, there are those that draw from both technical and fundamental analysis. I would say a good portion of forex traders fall in this category. Although, there is a definite bias. While forex traders can utilize both disciplines with success, they are more likely to favor one over the other. Most currency traders incorporate technical analysis more than they ever would fundamental analysis. Yet both are used.

In the end, every forex trader will find his or her "sweet spot" when it comes to analysis. This is based on a number of things such as personality, aversion to risk and their natural liking to either one of both the disciplines.

CHAPTER 11

THE TECHNICAL ANALYSIS

A simple definition of technical analysis is using past information to predict future movements. There are a number of different methods used in conducting this analysis, all of which rely on past movements.

Technical analysis is often linked to fundamental analysis. Technical analysis, however, places more of a focus of the effects of market movements rather than the causes. For traders who prefer to trade on intuition, the use of a technical analysis is often overlooked. But to the more informed trader, this method can be indispensable.

Technical indicators are used to collect and interpret past information to make predictions of future movements.

Charts, trends and mathematical techniques are used to examine aspects of a currency pair's price movement.

Charts can tell the story of a currency pair. The charted movement of a currency pair can provide a wealth of information, the historical movements and indicate likely future movements.

Trends can be derived from these charts, although there can be a different number of trend lines read. A basic trend line will show a currency pair is moving (or trending) whether it be upwards, downwards or sideways. Finding a trend line is often the most useful reading in predicting future movements of a currency pair.

Traders also often use resistance and support trend lines. A resistance trend line is indicated above the currency pair price. While a support trend line is indicated above the price. These trends lines are determined using the moving average lines, or more complex technical methods. Used in consideration of the projected trending of a currency pair, the support and resistance trend lines assist in predicting how the currency pair will move.

So why do traders use technical analysis? An accurate analysis is useful in finding the best entry and exit points for a profitable trade. The nature of the Forex market is face paced and highly volatile, so for many traders them technical analysis is a way of maintaining control over their trades and profitability.

The use of charts in this analysis clearly depicts for traders where momentum is rising, where a trend is forming, when a price is dropping and other useful events that may be developing. Technical indicators enable traders to accurately identify and exploit opportunities as they arise in the Forex market.

Because of its name, technical analysis is often perceived as an overly complex method of analysis. Technical analysis is not a difficult process. It does, however, require studying a number of different charts regularly and an awareness of technical indicators and how to use.

With the Internet, this process has also become much simpler with easier access to up to the minute information.

When starting out with technical analysis, it's easier to work with simpler charts projecting a smaller number of technical indicators. For example, only work with the indicators that give you a clear indication of the movements of a currency pair and its trend. It can become overwhelming and confusing when you start to clog your chart up with a number of different indicators. Focus on the trends and predicted movements of a currency pair to find your opportunities for trade entries and exits.

DISCUSSION OF TRADING METHODS

Never in my life have I seen anything like the plethora of methods which are coming on stream for the use in forecasting commodity prices. There are literally hundreds of techniques and approaches. This chapter will present rather briefly, but a few.

Some of them are rather conventional and this author will place an asterisk beside the ones which he personally uses. Listed in this chapter there are approximately thirty-six ways and means of forecasting prices. This does not take into consideration all the wonderful glorious little tidbits that come through the revelation of P&L charting technical analysis course.

(This author is very happy with P&L charting, for it enables this trader to quantify price action on a daily and intra-day basis. I know of no other system wherein each day's specific activity means more than the trend or congestion in which prices are trading. Each day's activity through the use of P&L charting portrays the evolution of a
trend or congestion, sometimes within one day.)

However, this author is most irritated by those traders who are convinced that their moving average, point and figure, resistance index, volume oscillator, balance volume, weighted moving averages, god knows what else, - basis, cash, - are the only system which is effective. And, that the system that they are using is the only one that will ever be effective and that they have no use for volume, open interest, seasonals, fundamentals, contrarian opinion, wave theories, point and figure, moving averages, oscillators, chart patterns, momentum indices, whatever, and are blindfolded to the evolution of anyone else's approach. (There. I got that off my chest.)

Often these traders do not even use their own systems and seem to me, at least, to be continually fighting the market. Assuming a trader has studied a technical analysis course and has a trading plan incorporating several methods of forecasting prices and combines them in a way which he can continually trade profits from the market, then this trader is worth listening to. In the section on planning, this author will succinctly portray his approaches to the market place and you will be surprised how flexible he is.

There are three basic methods to analyze the market behavior of commodity prices.

- fundamental
- mechanical
- technical

FUNDAMENTAL

Often the market goes completely contrary to fundamental considerations due to technical and other factors. The fundamental trader is interested in long range price movements and must be prepared to wait it out. Fundamentalists may deny it, but there are just too many external factors to be taken into account, such as the natural response to fundamental influences, reflected in the day by day fluctuations. So there's no need to seek them out for analysis. However, fundamentals underpin trend direction.

MECHANICAL

Mechanical methods use price and price alone to determine what action to take and this action does not require any decision on the part of the trader. There are three mechanical methods.

- chart
- computer summaries
- moving averages

Taking a technical analysis course will teach these rigid trading rules to be followed faithfully and it is usually based on some mathematical formula to predict the right time to trade. The computer tells you what a mathematical formula thinks you should do. One of the beauties of the mechanical method is they can be back checked. Computer oriented methods usually bias themselves towards mathematical trend analysis, using moving averages and other trading systems. The computer can be used as a chart reader and it can formulate and test any and all decision rules.

TECHNICAL

In the last several decades, a vast amount of work has been done to erect a means of technical tools, - all with the aim of anticipating futures prices from trading statistics, e.g. price, volume, O.I.

The technical approach from the simplest to the most complex and esoteric falls into four broad areas.

1. patterns on price charts
2. trend following methods
3. character of market analysis
4. structural theories.

There are many different methods for charting. The most popular are:
a) daily high/low/close bar charts
b) point and figure method
c) moving average of closing prices

The lists of approaches taken to technical analysis can be cataloged by the following technical approaches.

1. tape or board reading
2. price chart analysis - which consists of
    a) price trends
    b) support and resistance
    c) consolidation (continuation and reversal)
    d) price formations and patterns
    e) measurement rules
    f) wave theory

3. volume and open interest analysis
4. other technical indicators which are

In the last several decades, a vast amount of work has been done to erect a means of technical tools, - all with the aim of anticipating futures prices from trading statistics, e.g. price, volume, O.I.

The technical approach from the simplest to the most complex and esoteric falls into four broad areas.

1. patterns on price charts
2. trend following methods
3. character of market analysis
4. structural theories.

There are many different methods for charting. The most popular are:

a) daily high/low/close bar charts
b) point and figure method
c) moving average of closing prices

The lists of approaches taken to technical analysis can be cataloged by the following technical approaches.
1. tape or board reading
2. price chart analysis - which consists of
    a) price trends
    b) support and resistance
    c) consolidation (continuation and reversal)
    d) price formations and patterns
    e) measurement rules
    f) wave theory

3. volume and open interest analysis
4. other technical indicators which are:

a) measures of relative performance
b) study of periodic price performance
c) opinion survey and contrary opinion

In the world of foreign exchange, you will probably hear about technical analysis. It is just what the phrase means: you analyze and study the data with very technical or scientific means. You do not just give your own opinion, but you look at facts, study them, and then use them in formulas that can lead you to the result that you want.

In the case of foreign exchange, the result you want is the pattern that the trading makes in a given period. You want to use that pattern to make predictions. That is technical analysis explained at its simplest.

IS EVERYTHING ABOUT FOREX TECHNICAL ANALYSIS FACT-BASED?

Since there are data involved, technical analysis is mostly facts used in formulas. Numbers that result from a certain day of trading are facts that cannot be changed. Both people who have lost money and people who have gained money that day will have the same set of facts. It just so happens that their experiences about those facts are very different.

While Forex technical analysis may be fact-based, it is also based on a few assumptions. One of the main assumptions is that trading patterns will recur at regular intervals. In relation to this first assumption, another assumption arises, that is, currency value moves in trends.

Forex technical analysis is very fact-based that it does not bother itself much about generic guesses. The study no longer encompasses varying moods and opinions. It is as if the numbers have a life of their own, unaffected by outside influences.

HOW IS FOREX ANALYSIS DONE?

Technical analysis explained is about price charts and graphs. These mathematical representations are called studies. They are rightly called studies as you have to analyze these charts, graphs, and other forms of illustrated data to figure out what the trend is and what to expect in the next few days or even in the next 24 hours.

You take a certain timeline in foreign exchange trading of the currencies of your choice, and have to look at patterns that may emerge during that period. You can then base your predictions on those patterns. If you cannot find patterns on that smaller interval, you may have to extend your timeline.

WHAT MAKES FOREX TECHNICAL ANALYSIS EFFECTIVE?

Some may say that Forex analysis is just one way of finding patterns that can create market predictions. Its advantage is not exactly on the many formulas that can generate market predictions, but, specifically, the factual way of generating that prediction. The purely unemotional and objective way of arriving at the prediction is what makes it effective.

You may expect that traders who make use of this analysis will be more careful with making decisions on whether to buy or sell a currency. Emotional traders may immediately sell most or their entire share of a currency that suddenly rises but is expected to fall based on gut feeling.

Forex analysis should be best explained as objectively as it is. You should find someone who can teach you how to do it with charts, graphs, and the whole deal. If you want a comprehensive way of learning how to do technical analysis, then you should undergo technical analysis training.

WHY FUNDAMENTAL ANALYSIS & TECHNICAL ANALYSIS ARE THE SAME

For years, I have been asked this same question over and over again, "Which is better, fundamental analysis or technical analysis?".

For decades, analysts of one camp argued about the ineffectiveness of the other and provided reasons and evidences how one method of analysis can be used at the exclusion of the other. For decades, fundamental analysts; people who dig deep into the business model and financial statements of companies, gave proof to the ineffectiveness of technical analysis. For decades too have technical analysts; people who read charts to find trends, patterns and investor behaviors, gave proof to the ineffectiveness of fundamental analysis.

Suddenly, it feels like there are 2 different worlds existing simultaneously, talking about the same stocks, same markets with views that are supposed to have nothing to do with one another. How is that possible?

If fundamental analysis is truly ineffective, why have fundamental analysis existed for so many centuries? If technical analysis is truly ineffective, why are technical analysis and chartists still paid so much money in Wall Street? If fundamental analysis is ineffective, why does earnings releases move stocks so much? If technical analysis is ineffective, why do resistance levels and support levels prove to be accurate time and time over again? What if both methods are truly one and the same thing?

Yes, fundamental analysis and technical analysis are really two sides of the same coin, two perspectives on the same issue and two components making up a full picture.

Fundamental analysis explores 2 main issues; Earnings expectation and Growth expectations. The ultimate objective of fundamental analysis is to arrive at an opinion on the future profitability of a company and how much that profitability is worth in terms of stock price. The higher the earnings expectations and growth expectations, the higher the stock price ought to be. However, scientific as this may be, it is missing the final element that moves stocks... investor sentiments or how much investors think that earnings and growth expectation is ultimately worth! Technical analysis reflects the final verdict of investors towards that earnings and growth expectation. Without this final verdict, all analysis is meaningless. However, this final verdict may not always be inline with your own expectation towards the future profitability and growth of a company. Because both fundamental analysis and technical analysis is really the same thing, a decision to buy or sell a stock should take both views into consideration. When fundamental analysis revealed a potential rise in earnings, does the charts support that view? Have investors started moving ahead of the news? Does the trend so far reveal that investors are not impressed with that outlook at all? When a reversal signal turns up in technical analysis, is there any fundamental reasons driving that reversal? Is it just nothing but an unsustainable exuberance not supported by fundamental reasons?

That being said, when a company's fundamental outlook is continuously strong over a long period of time, technicals will also reflect that same long term strength through long term bullish trend and patterns.

In this sense, fundamental analysis and fundamental analysis are truly one and the same and nobody can do with one and not the other. It is like examining the physical attributes of a boxer versus his track record. You cannot have a complete picture of the capabilities of a boxer unless you take both views into consideration.

Because fundamental analysis and technical analysis are 2 different views on the same subject, they both have certain strengths over each other.

Fundamental analysis is capable of telling if a company has long term growth potential and whether or not its stocks are worth while long term investments. However, fundamental analysis is incapable of predicting or explaining short term trends of a few days that are not caused by fundamental company events like earnings release. Technical analysis on the other hand is capable of telling when prices are out of sorts and when prices shouldn't rise or fall anymore using support and resistance levels. Such knowledge is extremely useful in trading short term trends. However, technical analysis has proved to be ineffective at predicting long term price actions as business fundamentals does change significantly from year to year.

I hope I have resolved the feud between fundamental and technical analysis today and that you have understood that both are really the same thing, talking about the same thing while providing a slightly different perspective. I hope you will embrace both methods from now on and use the right bias on the right investment horizon and outlook.

CHAPTER 12

THE RISK-REWARD RATIO

If you are a trader of Stocks and/or Commodities, you have heard mentioned from various sources and so-called educators something called the "Risk/Reward Ratio". According to one source, "Risk/Reward Ratio" is defined as;

"A ratio used by many investors to compare the expected returns of an investment to the amount of risk undertaken to capture these returns."

Evaluating risk is always an important part of investing and speculating. Before a trade is taken, it is prudent to determine if the risk is appropriate for the amount of available capital and whether there is good potential for reward by taking that risk.

For many, the determination of whether a trade is worth taking is based on some hard and fast rule that the expected reward should be a certain increment of the risk. This is what many call the "Risk/Reward Ratio". For example, if the trader expects a trade will likely produce at least double the amount risked, this would be referred to as a 2:1 Risk/Reward Ratio. Many look for this ratio to be at least 3:1 before taking the trade.

Oddly enough, the ratio itself does not match the description. For instance, a 3:1 Risk/Reward Ratio is meant to mean that the trade has the potential to produce profits that are three times greater than the risk. Seen in that light, however, should it not be called the Reward/Risk Ratio instead? By reference of Risk/Reward, you'd at least think traders would state the risk first followed by the expected profit potential. Unfortunately, this is not the case in the general trading populace.

In any event, should trades be determined by such a ratio? While it is not difficult to decide on a percentage of overall funds that may be risked in order to follow a strict Money-Management plan, should the determination of whether to risk at all be laid upon the expectation that a trade will produce a certain multiple of risk?

When you consider that it is virtually impossible to determine profit in advance, it all comes down to basing your decision to trade on an estimation. One definition of 'estimate' is;

"A judgment based on one's impressions; an opinion."

How far is that from "guessing"?

Well, the difference is minor, but 'estimating' does imply that you have a tad more information to work with in order to arrive at an 'opinion', where 'guessing' usually based on "little or no information". But the difference is indeed small. Another way of saying 'estimation' is to say an "educated" guess.

When we consider that the 'Reward' component of the "Risk/Reward Ratio" is a function of taking an 'educated guess', should our trading decisions be based on such a loosely defined criteria?

Rather than base a trade on the amount of profit 'you think' you will gain from taking a trade, the decision should be based on the simple expectation of whether you expect a profit at all. The amount of profit should be left up to the market and whether you manage the trade effectively once it has commenced. However, it never hurts to at least get an idea of what the market may provide in potential profits at a minimum.
While no method of 'estimating' potential profit is foolproof, we can logically make some pretty good 'educated' guesses. The following three examples should provide you with a good idea on how to go about this.

We start by first determining whether a potential trade exists without regard to the amount of potential profit. This determination can be based on various factors that you have found effective. Since I am mostly familiar with my own way of timing the markets, we'll simply have to go with that.
The first determination is whether the market is 'correcting'. Another term for this is a trend "pullback". In our first example (Chart 1), we can see that prices had been rising after breaking above a downward trend line that had been containing a bearish trend. This rise in price also successfully exceeded a previous swing top that was one of the tops used for that declining trend line. This, as W. D. Gann would say, was the first signal that a "change in trend" was likely occurring.

Then the market started to decline again. This is our trend 'pullback/correction'. Up to this point, anyone with A price chart and the ability to draw trend lines can accomplish this. At this point,

129

however, the method you use to time the market and the method I use may differ.

So I will refer to my own method and you can replace that language with your own.

Somewhere along this 'correction' it has been determined that there is very good potential for the retracement to end and for prices to start rising again. My determining this is with the use of cycle turn dates that allows for being within a single price bar accuracy of calculating when a market turn is likely. Confirmation of this expectation will then commit me into the trade. Before taking the trade, however, the risk is evaluated. What might my risk be?

Considering that the expectation is for the retracement to have ended and that a swing bottom is highly likely at this time, and in addition that I will not commit to the trade unless the swing bottom confirms, my risk in this example would be the range of that swing bottom price bar. Therefore, in advance, I would know what my 'risk' would be.

HOW ABOUT THE REWARD?

Again looking at Chart 1, note that the "minimum potential profit" is determined to be the point on the price chart where the retracement began. So if my trade entry is at price "A" and the correction started at "B", the 'minimum' estimated 'reward' would be from "A" to "B" in points.
If this 'minimum' profit potential is acceptable for the amount of risk being taken, then the trade can be initiated. But it should be

understood that this is simply the 'minimum' potential estimated. There is always the possibility, if you allow for it, to make greater profits. Also, by managing your stop-loss effectively, you can be reducing your risk exposure along the way. As your stop-loss is adjusted during the course of the trade, your risk shrinks and your profit potential continues to be a product of what the market is willing to provide.

Once your minimum profit target has been reached, you can continue to 'estimate' new logical targets. Chart 2 shows how you can get your next profit estimation. The technique here is to simply take the initial wave (range) that was used for your first profit estimate and add this range to where the retracement had ended. This is often referred to as an "Alternate-Expansion".

If your trade continues to do well and that 'alternate' expansion level is reached, and assuming you have not been stopped out or prematurely exited your trade, you can then perform an 'extended' profit estimation. The technique is the same as the 'alternate' expansion technique just discussed, except that the initial 'wave' (range) is added to itself as shown in Chart 3.

While these are very useful approaches to help determine 'reward', keep in mind that they are still 'educated' guesses at best. Do not get hung up on basing your trades on some fixed Risk/Reward Ratio as a means to determine whether a trade should be taken, but to simply determine first whether you have a potential trade and then determine whether the minimum amount of 'likely' profit would make the trade worth the risk in your opinion.

ONLINE TRADING- HOW TO SET YOUR RISK-REWARD RATIO

Online trading in the Forex market is increasing and the traders like to trade EURUSD, USDJYP and GPBUSD. The EURUSD is the most traded currency pairs in the world. The spread between the buying and selling price is at the most online trading platforms 2 pips. The small spread means that the trader faster generate profit at the EURUSD than at the GPBUSD where the spread between the buying and selling price is 4 pips.

The objective in this chapter is the risk-reward ratio. The risk-reward ratio is the ratio of the risk and reward in a trade. The goal is to describe the risk-reward ratio in deep.

The risk and reward ratio. The reward is the expected return in profit when the trader enters a trade. The risk is the changes in the currency rate. If the trader wants to invest in a trade and the invested capital is 200 Euro the expected return should not be less than 400 Euro. The risk is 200 Euro and the reward is 400 Euro. The risk-reward ratio is 1:2. For a beginner in the Forex market the ratio should not be less than 1:3. In the mentioned trade the reward should be 600 Euro for a beginner.

A Forex trader is interested in profit and therefore also interested in trading more currency pairs at the same time or trade more trades during the day. A trader that takes currency trading seriously will also consider the risk-reward ratio for all the trades he enters.

If a trader expects that the profit during a day will be 50 pips per trade and has set the stop/loss at 25 pips his ratio is 1:2. The trader has planned a day containing of 3 trades and expects 50% of them to yield a profit.

If the day is as planned the day will gain a profit of 75 pips. The calculation is 3 times 50 pips and will gain 150 pips. The stop/loss is calculated to 3 times 25 pips and the loss will be 75 pips. The profit is 150 pips minus 75 pips and as written 75 pips.

If the day consists of 2 extra trades and there is a loss on the them the profit is 2 times 25 pips which is a loss of 50 pips. The overall profit is at the end of the trading day 15 pips. The 75 pips already earned minus the 50 pips for the 2   losses.

Conclusion. Trading Forex online is about planning and setting the risk-reward ratio at a reasonable level. As the example in the article illustrates is a wide ratio for a beginner in the Forex market important because the chances to gain a profit is big even if the planned trades doesn't go as planned.

USE YOUR RISK/REWARD RATIO TO BE MORE PROFITABLE

An extremely successful way to determine exit points is to look at the risk/reward ratio on a trade. Applying the risk/reward ratio provides a pre-set and well calibrated exit points. If the trade doesn't offer a favorable risk/reward, then the trade should be avoided, which helps to eliminate any low-quality trades from being taken.

If the target is reached on a trade, then the position will be closed, and the target priced according to the strategy in place. If the stop loss is reached, then the manageable loss will be accepted, and the trade will be closed before it has the opportunity to become a larger loss. With this, there isn't any confusion regarding what to do, an exit has been planned for the predetermined exit points, regardless of if it is unprofitable or profitable.

If the trend is up during a trade, then buying during a pullback is recommended. In some cases, waiting for the price to consolidate for several bars or candlesticks, and then buying when the price exceeds the high of consolidation is best. The difference between entry and stop loss is significant enough to see, making it possible to know what to do, and when.

In theory, the risk/reward model is both effective and simple. The real challenge occurs when a person tries to make it work altogether. It doesn't really matter how good the reward:risk is if the price doesn't ever make it to the profit target. A quality target, that has a favorable risk/reward will also require a quality entry technique. The stop loss and entry will determine the risk portion of the equation, so the lower the risk is, then the easier it will be to have a more favorable risk/reward scenario. Note that the loss shouldn't be so small that the stop loss is triggered unnecessarily.

While this may sound confusing, it is easier to understand with a real-world scenario. Assume that you are making a swing trade and purchase a currency pair with a profit target of 60 pips. Then, a reasonable the stop loss is set at 25-30 pips. In this case, only 25-30 pips just above or below your support or resistance levels, will give you a 2 to 1 reward to risk as a realistic expectation.

The actual calculation of the risk/reward ratio is contingent on the currency pair that is being traded and, due to the many pre-existing variables in the calculation of the pip value for a trade, it is easier explained with stocks to use a fixed value. If you enter a trade for a stock that is priced at $50 USD, your target is $55, and your stop loss

is set at $1, the stock will only have to move by 10 percent to reach
the $55 mark, or two percent tom reach the stop loss, which creates a
5:1 reward:risk.

Depending on market conditions and the economic calendar, there
are quite a few currency pair that will move by 10 percent in just a
week or two. I would never set a trade with a 1/1 risk/reward ration
and would always go for a 2:1 or a 3:1 reward:risk. This means a
bigger move is needed to achieve the target, but makes the risk worth
entering the trade.

To be successful, a trader have to find a setup that helps to produce a
high risk/reward ratio. However, it is necessary to have a relatively
conservative price to produce the desired ratios.

CHAPTER 13

TYPES OF ORDERS

Individuals attempting to get into the foreign exchange market must
have an understanding of the best times in which to negotiate deals.
Besides being closed on the weekends, the forex trading is kind of like

shopping at a convenience store: the market's open 24 hours per day. While this means that you could try forex trading any time, day or night, realistically that will not always work out to your benefit. There are actually peak hours in which different currencies are ideal for FX trading and learning them is crucial to properly executing a successful transaction.

WHAT IS THE BEST TIME FOR FOREX TRADING?

The optimal time for a forex broker to execute a currency exchange is when the market is at its most active. At these daily pinnacles, the market has the greatest activity and therefore has the most volume of trades available. These peak trading hours coincide with the overlap of each particular currency's trading market being open. Although forex trading is open 24 hours per day, each country's individual market opens and closes in 8 hour cycles.

This means, for example, that the New York market is never open at the same time as the Tokyo market. But there are periods throughout the day when two markets are open simultaneously, which means more active brokers making more trades, allowing for a better probability that a particular trade will find a partner to complete the transaction.

Working within these hours increases the chances of making successful trade. Attempting to make deals outside of these overlap periods is a waste of time. Turn off the computer and try again later.

FOREX TRADING HOURS

These are the hours for the top country's trading markets in Eastern Standard Time (EST).

Region, City, Opens (EST), Closes (EST)
Europe, London, 3:00 am, 12:00 noon
America, New York, 8:00 am, 5:00 pm
Asia, Tokyo, 7:00 pm, 4:00 am
Pacific, Sydney, 5:00 pm, 2:00 am

FOREX TRADING OVERLAP

Of the four major FX markets, these are the overlaps in sessions in EST.
New York and London: 8:00 am to 12:00 noon
Sydney and Tokyo: 7:00 pm to 2:00 am
London and Tokyo: 3:00 am to 4:00 am

WHAT THIS MEANS

These overlaps mean that trading currencies during these periods are going to yield the best results. As an example, if someone wanted to trade Euros (EUR) for United States dollars (USD), then the best time to accomplish this is from 8:00 am- 12:00 noon EST when London's and New York's markets are open.

During these overlapping forex trading sessions, the volume of trades is greatest, increasing the likelihood of a deal being done and a profit being turned.

DIFFERENT TYPES OF ORDER

An order is an instruction from the trader to the forex broker to either buy or sell on an exchange. There are different types of orders that can be made. Here are a few common orders:

Market Order: An order to buy or sell immediately at the current market price.

Stop-Loss Order: An order intending to cut off losses at a predetermined price.

Limit Entry Order: An order to sell above the market at a specified level, or purchase below the market at a specified level, under the belief that once the price hits that specified level, it will reverse directions.

Stop-Entry Order: An order to sell above the market or purchase below the market at a specified level, with the belief that the price will maintain its current trend and continue in the same direction.

One Cancels Other (OCO) Order: An order that if one is instructed to follow, it cancels another order.

Good Till Canceled (GTC) Order: An order that stays available in the market until it is either accepted or canceled.

THE TYPE OF ORDERS YOU CAN PLACE

Forex trading is all about entering orders into the currency market and enter these orders well and with all the knowledge you can possible have of the market so you can expect to have a profit from each of these orders. Maybe you won't be successful every time but with the right trading system you can profit most of the time from your trades.

Respect to the orders you can use as a forex trader, there are three type of orders that are available for you to use. These are the Stop Order, Limit Order and Market Order.

Before you venture out in the Forex markets it will do you good to learn a method that yields instant profits. The Forex trading courses offered from Forex mentors can reveal the intricacies of the Forex market and teach you how to place orders that will make your profit run through the roof.

The Forex trading courses should also teach you the type of orders and how to use them to your advantage. Here is a general preview of the various types of orders that you can use.

Marker Order: This order you use to directly enter or exit the market at a given point and time at the quoted price. You can buy a currency pair at the ask price or sell it at the bid price.This kind of order is used for the purpose of selling or buying a currency pair at the market price being used at the instant the order arrives to the brokers "hands" which is usually within a few seconds or even less after you hit the enter key in your trading station.

After you have used a market order then it's time for you to consider using stop and limit orders. These are two kind of orders that are useful for the purpose of your own security as a forex trader. This means that by using this kind of orders you will be making sure that you won't be losing more money than you can afford to lose (of course you should always aim to lose the less amount possible, but bad trades can happen and that's why you have this kind of orders).

Limit Order: This order is used to buy or sell at a price of your choice. A buy limit order is placed at a price lower than the existing price and will be filled only if the price falls below to that level. A sell limit order is the opposite and will be filled only when the price of the pair rises to the limit price you have indicated. A limit order is also a limit that takes you out of the market, but in this case is a positive limit, with this I mean that you are using a limit order to specify the minimum amount you are willing to earn from a given trade. Once you reach this point you are out of the market with good profits in your hands and without risking you capital in an unnecessary way.

Stop Order: A stop order is defined as a previously set limit in your trading position that will take you out of the market as soon as the price of the given currency pair you are trading at the moment touches a pricing point (above or below your entering point depending if you are buying or selling) that is the most you are willing to lose in that trade. It's kind of a safety valve that will close your position without you having the risk of losing all of your account in just one bad trade. It is used to buy or sell at a predetermined price. A buy stop order will be activated if the market trades at or above the stop price. Conversely, a sell buy order will be activated when the market trades at or below the predetermined stop price.

Forex trading courses are not limited to knowing the types of orders that you can use, there is a lot more to them and it is quite a tricky job to trade Forex.

CHAPTER 14

HOW MANY PIPS IS ENOUGH

This chapter will explain how even a relatively new and inexperienced trader can easily gain 10 or more pips a day on average -- by observing and taking advantage of a common market behavioral pattern during the daily New York Close, or from 2 p.m to 4 p.m. Eastern time (New York time).

Once a trader has observed the forex market for a length of time, he or she will recognize that the market does have certain habits and does frequently repeat daily patterns of activity. Learning these patterns and recognizing these habits does not require any special knowledge, training or education. All it takes is careful observation and looking for patterns as to how the market tends to behave during certain times of the trading day. As a new trader, if you spend enough time observing the market movements with respect to time of day, you will begin to see some regular predictable patterns.

One of the market's predictable habits occurs in the New York afternoon, after 2 pm EST and into the final New York daily closing. Most notably, this pattern is most frequently observed in the EUR/USD. During this time of the trading day, trading flows are usually light and volatility is low. One pattern that has been very consistent over time, for whatever reason, is that there tends to be a pivot that becomes apparent sometime just after 2 pm EST. By "pivot," I am referring to a "pullback" or "retracement" from the overall day's predominant trend.

In other words, if the trend of the day for the EUR/USD has been rising, then between 2 pm and 3:30 pm EST, the market will typically see a pullback lower, usually around 20 to 30 pips. On the other hand, if the daily trend for the EUR/USD has been downward, then after 2 pm a retracement of 20-30 pips higher is often observed.

By checking the market or checking the charts in the New York afternoon around 2 pm Eastern time, a new and even an inexperienced trader may recognize this pattern and then safely execute a high probability trade. If a person is available to trade at this time of day on a consistent basis, they could expect to gain an average of 10 pips a day with a fair amount of ease.

MAKE 100 PIPS DAILY WITH A VERY SIMPLE SET AND FORGET FOREX STRATEGY - IDEAL FOR THOSE WITH 9-5 JOBS

Do you want to make 100 Pips Daily? If you can really make 100 pips every day, it means 3,000 pips every month. 1 pips is equal to $10 on a standard lot. 3,000 pips a   month translates into $30,000. Not bad, huh? Well, Karl Dittmann wants to help you with his very simple 100 Pips

Daily- Set & Forget Forex Trading Strategy that can help you make 100 pips daily easily.

Karl Dittmann from Bonn, Germany is a veteran trader who has been making a living trading differet markets successfully. He has been releasing very simple trading systems that have helped traders all over the world to trade different market successfully and make money.

100   Pips Daily-Set & Forget Forex Trading Strategy is another mechanical forex trading system that Karl uses everyday to make 100

pips daily. This is a 100% pure mechanical forex trading system that is ideal for those with a 9-5 job. Everyday millions of people around the world attempt to make money trading forex. Most of them keep on losing money.

This simple Set & Forget Strategy can help those people a lot. Two principles that have worked in trading always is good money management and secret market timing. 30 years of experience trading different markets has taught Karl the importance of using proper money system and utilizing secret market timing. This manual trading strategy uses both!

This Set & Forget Strategy does not need you to monitor the market. Most trading systems depend on using chart patterns. Identifying a chart pattern is a difficult process that requires some experience trading the market. In the same way, trading support and resistance or pivot points also need practice and experience. This is a unique price driven strategy that uses no indicators, no chart patterns, no support and resistance and no pivots. You will be amazed to discover how simple this 100 Pips Daily-Set and Forget Forex Trading Strategy is! You can learn it easily and use it to trade the forex market the very same day.
So what is this Set & Forget Strategy. This 100 Pips Daily-Set Forget Strategy requires you to open the chart at a specific time, Place a few orders and that's it, you are done! You don't have to do anything else or monitor the trade anymore. You will automatically earn 100 pips in a few minutes or hours. It is as simple as that. You only need $250 in your trading account to start using this simple forex trading strategy.

What you need to do is test this forex strategy on your demo account for a few days and see how easily it makes 100 pips for you every daily. The price of this product is only $54. Compare this with other forex systems that are being sold for hundreds of dollars. Karl says he makes enough money trading so he does not need to make money by selling his products. He has only released this 100 Pips Daily - Set &

Forget Forex Trading Strategy to help people to stop losing money and start making money with forex!

It matters NOT how many Pips you manage to make day in day out. What matters most is HOW you make those Pips. And by this we do not mean that it matters what market you trade, when you trade, how often you trade, how sizeable your trading balance is, etc. No, it's much more straight forward than that.

"Newbies" (a word we personally hate) regularly get roped in by sales and promotional hype with headlines like 100 Pips A Day, 500 Pips A Week, etc. The hype more often than not illustrates endless successful trades, "unsolicited" testimonials, falsified performance together with endless peddling by 3rd parties interested only in lining their own pockets.

We are not implying that all those selling systems do this however there are many that do. But, even if we can trust the enticing headlines we need ask just one primary question and apply some basic maths to tell us a lot of more of what we REALLY need to know.

Below we have specified two hypothetical Trading systems, however they could just as easily be real. Both trade cable (GBPUSD) and are Simple once a day Set & Forget Trading systems. Which one would you choose?

System 1 - 500 pips per week
So, just follow this strategy, trade at just GBP1 a point and bring in GBP500 a week or GBP2,000 a month. Impressive enough, until we ask our primary question:

-    What is the Risk:Reward per trade?

System 2 operates as follows. You risk 2,000 Pips on each trade to make 500, a huge Risk:Reward of 4:1. That's the only answer we need.

Now, we translate this into actual money, it's relatively Simple.
To make GBP500 a week (based on the headline claim of 500 Pips) we will have to risk GBP2,000 on each trade. Adopting the industry standard Risk profile of 2% per trade that means we require a starting account balance of GBP100,000.
System 2 - 200 pips a month

Only 200 Pips a month! Sounds a little mean based on the fact System 1 returns 2,000 Pips a month (10 times more). However, System 2 has a Risk:Reward per trade of 1:2, it risks 20 Pips per trade to make 40.

To compare apples with apples let's assume that System 1 does work and delivers 2,000 pips a month, the actual GBP2,000 a month at GBP1 a point mentioned previously.

For System 2 to return this same amount each month, we need to divide GBP2,000 by 200, the number of Pips made each month. This means we have to trade at GBP10 a Pip as a result risking GBP200 per trade.

So, Which product Is The better

The answer is most likely already obvious however some basic maths makes it clear.

To use System 1 we have previously worked out that we need a starting account balance of GBP100,000. We risk 2% per trade, GBP2,000 to make GBP500 a week or, GBP2,000 a month. A return of 2% a month.

System 2 risks GBP200 (GBP10 a Pip) per trade so based on 2% risk per trade this means we need a starting account balance of just GBP10,000. If we accomplish our 200 Pips every month it equates to the same return as System 1 (GBP2,000) however in this instance we are looking at a 20% return per month, in relation to our starting account balance.

Not sure yet? There is one further bit of maths you can do to check the validity of a product. What happens if I have 5 losers in a row, don't think it can't, it can and it will. Well, with System 1 we will end up with a GBP10,000 drawdown, with System 2, just GBP1,000. In both scenarios this equates to 10% of our account balance.

HOW YOU CAN PROFIT AT LEAST 200 PIPS EACH WEEK TRADING FOREX

Profiting 200 pips from the forex market might seem rather out-of-reach for most (including yourself perhaps) if you have not been there done that. This logic is very simple to understand here - Considering a trader who can consistently nail an average of 200 pips from the forex market each week, this kind of profit target would not be overwhelming to him/her anymore. On the other hand, if you are the kind of trader who struggle to make 50 - 80 pips each week, this target of 200 pips might seem like an impossible target for you (at least for now). However, nothing is hard or impossible as long as you break down everything and try to understand the process in a simple manner - Likewise for this strategy on profiting 200 pips each week.

Let me share the details below:

In forex trading, being "consistent " is really the key to succeed continuously month after month and for a long time to come. Nothing beats this fact I am sure. So instead of thinking how to make 200 pips each week, you just have to break it down into 40 pips a day instead. Not only is 40 pips a very achievable target, but it is also a " realistic " target as well. Why do I say so?

Because for almost all the currency pairs available for trading, their average daily pips range would be between 100   - 150 pips at least. Hence, when you are aiming for just 40 pips out of this range, it is definitely very do-able once you understand some proven facts I am sharing here. For this example, let me use the EUR/USD for my explanation of this strategy. This is one of the most commonly traded pair and the liquidity is definitely good.

Here are some tips for you to secure the 40 pips target with confidence:

1) Always Trade On The Bigger Time-frames Such As 1 hourly or 4 hourly

By looking at the bigger time-frames, you are actually looking at the " bigger " price projection in the market. Therefore, not only are you looking at more reliable signals & patterns formation from the chart, but also not that tiring after all as compared to staring at the 1 minute or 5 minutes charts instead.

2) You Should Trade With A Good " Risk/Reward " Ratio Of At Least 1.5x

Forex trading is merely a game of probability after all. As long as you lose less than what you win each time and simply rinse and repeat over many trades, you are going to be in the "positive" profits zone every month. So by applying a risk/reward ratio of 1.5x, you would plan your take profit at 45 pips (applicable for a pair such as EUR/USD) each time and stop loss at 30 pips. When you stick strictly to this ratio, each time you would win 45 pips but when you lose, it is only 30 pips. Lose less and win more - That's what I called it!

3) Learn Forex Trading Strategies For Both Sideway & Trending Market

In the forex market, it is either the market is going sideway (ranging) OR trending. And the beauty is that you can definitely nail those pips (profits) you need from both market condition once you have some strategies for each different market.

To truly put all odds on your side, it is no good to apply just one strategy to all market conditions as in this way, you would not be getting good results in the long run or maybe only "breakeven " perhaps. So what you should do is to include good strategies meant for both the sideway & trending market in your trading basket. And the best strategies you should use would be based on Price Action itself.

Why so?

This is because Price Action is not lagging and the " hints " you derive from the actual market Price Action is more reliable most of the time. On the other hand, when you rely too heavily on the so called " textbook technical indicators", you would suffer more confusions and uncertainty as they are generally plain lagging and not as reliable as compared to Price Action.

Having stick to these 3 proven tips, your effort to make 200 pips each week would not be such a challenge anymore. You would suffer some losses definitely, but if you trade just 2 times a day (using TP 45 pips & SL 30 pips) and your strategies are just 50% accurate - 200 Pips by the end of the week is very do-able indeed! So if you are keen on tuning both your mindset and trading skills to make 200 pips each week, do try out and get familiar with these 3 rules using a DEMO account first.

Once you can " consistently " get many repeated 200 pips each week, you can then proceed onto a Live trading account if you want. 200 pips each week would roughly equate to about 800 pips every month. Now do you know how much these kind of pips would help to grow your account size by only risking 2 -3 % each time? I would say, it is enough to make most traders around the world "filled with envy " once they know about your success with forex!

In closing, I must state the obvious disclaimer - that trading forex is a risky endeavor with no guarantees. Trade with caution and never trade more than you can afford to lose. Spend time observing the market to recognize its patterns so you may make smart, high probability trades and minimize risks.

Conclusion

We pay wise attention to this Simple formula when conducting all of our Trading system and Signal service reviews. In reality, on occasion, we have chosen not to go ahead with a review after carrying out these simple sums. We believe every trader, especially those new to trading, adopt a comparable routine.

CHAPTER 15

TRADING PSYCHOLOGY

Many aspiring Forex traders find themselves frightened of joining the ranks due to common misconception that Forex trading is too difficult or even worse - a losing game. This is quite frankly not true.

Another way to say it would be that by applying several very easy to implement techniques, the Forex trading game could be effortlessly conquered.

The way that I see it and throughout my experience as a Forex coach these techniques have everything to do with the trader's mindset. I like to refer to these techniques as Forex trading psychology. It has been said that trading psychology accounts for 90% of a trader's success. I find this to be absolutely true.

In this Chapter I wish to address several of what I find to be the most important concepts that every Forex trader needs to address. Applying these techniques will make a positive difference in any trader's overall performance; fully understanding these techniques will make any trader successful for life regardless of what the market does.

In Forex trading 95% of traders lost 50 years ago and 95% lose today and this is despite all the advances we have seen in technology and forecasting in the period and the reason the same number lose, is because they cannot get the right mindset to succeed and this article is all about getting the right mindset for success.

Forex Trading Psychology, is so important because when you trade Forex you have to adopt a mindset which is not common in everyday life and here, we will go through all the different areas you need to master and the good news is anyone can do it and win.

In life were taught to trust experts and they do a job you pay them and that's it job done. In FX trading most of the people who sell expert advice, don't make money and top of the list are the Forex robot and Forex Expert Advisors. Your supposed to believe that by following these cheap software packages, you will make an income for life with no effort but they all lose, because the fact is Forex trading success relies on taking responsibility for your actions - the only person who can give you success is you.

Psychology is one of the weirdest areas of forex trading. You can be making perfect trades most of the time on your demo account but as soon as there's real money on the table - even if it's on the tiniest of trades - your system goes to pot and your bank starts to evaporate. If that's the case with you, it's time to examine your forex trading psychology and see how you can improve it.

In normal everyday life being wrong is not seen as a good trait but in Forex trading your going to be wrong and you have to accept it and not only that you will lose money when you do! However keeping losses small in Forex trading is the very key to success, fail to keep your losses small and you will end up in the majority of losers.

Working hard and being clever in normal life is seen as an admirable trait but in Forex trading it doesn't bring you success, simple systems work best and you don't need to work hard to make money, you need to work smart.
You also need the confidence and courage to make big gains and most traders bank their profits to soon but do this and you won't cover your losing trades.

FX trading involves working smart and getting a good education and then trading a simple system with discipline and if you do this you will succeed. The traders who think technology and hard work are needed to win are wrong. All you need is a simple system and the right attitude and you can enjoy Forex trading success.

One final thought 50 years ago 95% of traders lost money and today they do so, how many will lose in 50 years time?

If you answered 95%, you will see how important Forex Trading Psychology is in terms of achieving success so get the right mindset and win.

Understanding the right Forex trading psychology can and will help you learn to avoid becoming one of the majority of traders that enter the Forex trading market and end up failing. The number one reason behind such failures is a lack of proper psychological preparation. In other words, currency traders that are not prepared to face and even accept the fact that not having control over things means having to accept a higher risk.

Apply the Right Psychology

The truth is that foreign exchange trading is more about applying the right psychology than using the right methods. Once you accept this fact, you will be well on your way to succeeding as an FX trader. Failing to understand Forex trading psychology can and does mean that you will be more prone to succumbing to fear and confusion as well as become desperate when making trades. This can lead to a series of losses. The methods you apply will be hard to follow because you will become overcome with fear.

Critical Factor

All this only goes to show that trading psychology is the most critical factor that can either make or break you as a currency investor. When an investor starts losing money on a regular basis they will become obsessed with finding out why they are such pathetic losers. They will start doubting their trade methods and the problem will worsen with each bad experience. This can ultimately lead them to quit the foreign exchange market altogether.

This need not be the case for those who learn about and apply the right Forex trading psychology plan. The fact of the matter is that to succeed in FX requires having the right plan as well as the right psychology or mindset. Without proper mindset, a trader will not have much of a chance to transition from fear and emotion-based trading to trading according to their chosen plan.
Without the right trading psychology, traders will also not succeed in being objective when assessing and understanding their plans and this will then lead them down the path of failure instead of helping them walk the path to success.
Assess Events Honestly

The right Forex trading psychology is one that is based on making honest assessments and accepting events that have already taken place. The right plan must have the following components:

-        Acceptance that losses are a normal part of the FX business
-        Avoiding too much focus on losing/winning and being objective about following a plan
-        Being neutral as well as non judgmental about oneself
-        Accepting that emotions are a natural part of life
-        Making a slow but steady start

It is also important to understand that currency trading occurs in an environment which offers unique challenges that include:

-   Markets are powerful
-   Odds are stacked against you
-   Absence of any rule of law; so, make your own rules
-   Work ethics do not count for anything

- Being very clever also does not count for anything

All these factors show that unless you apply the right rules and act with discipline, success in the foreign exchange business will elude you. Remember also that a good strategy is just one part of the roadmap to success in the currency market.

The bottom line is that with both a strategy and the right Forex trading psychology plan, it becomes much easier to succeed in this business. The right mindset will help you join the ranks of the traders that win at the FX game. Being emotional will condemn you to perpetually being a loser.

The psychology of a Forex investor is vital for success. The wrong Forex trading psychology can lead to failure. Emotions must be kept aside and the trader must have an objective plan and stick to it. This article discusses the mindset that a currency trader must have in order to be successful.

THINK IN PIPS

The amount of pips you risk on a trade will stay near enough constant regardless of the size of your bank.

This is actually a very important psychological barrier to overcome. Early on in your trading career you'll almost certainly be concentrating on how much money you're staking and (hopefully) making. But as you get more successful, the size of your trades will naturally increase. And then your conscious mind kicks in and conspires against you, causing you to make novice-like mistakes even though you're experienced.

If you've just started trading this can be even worse. Even the smallest stake feels as though your entire life savings are riding on this trade being a success. At least translating it into pips makes any nagging worries and doubts slightly more abstract.

BECOME A ROBOT

Whilst many than they do as robotic as forex robots make more for their creators for traders, the idea of making your trading possible helps a lot.

The more you can detach your personality from your trading the better. Our ego is often the only thing that stands between us and an every growing bank.

If you find yourself kicking yourself when you examine those trades where you quit too early or moved your stop loss before your own trading rules really allowed you to then becoming more robot like will help improve your forex trading psychology.

Less is more I know you're probably thinking that this is a contradiction in terms. After all, if you can make more trades then surely you can make more profit?

That's true if every trade you take has a high chance of working out. But if you go back and examine your recent trades, there's a good chance that you took some "on the fly" even though they didn't tick every possible box they should have done. Then you find you're kicking yourself when you go back and examine them.

So discipline yourself to take less trades - only the ones that totally fit the system you're following.

And while you're at it, cut down on the number of pairs you're trading. Yes, less is more works here as well.

Instead of trying to be an expert in three or more pairs, cut down to two or - better yet - just one pair.

You'll probably need to go cold turkey when you do this but after a few days of just watching one pair you'll be kicking yourself and asking yourself why you didn't make this a part of your forex trading psychology earlier.

- A SUCCESSFUL FOREX TRADER ALWAYS TRADES WITH A PRE-DETERMINED PLAN.

A trader that has fixed goals and a method that is back-tested and proven to earn realistic returns over the long term is many steps ahead of a trader that trades based on gut feelings or a method that has variables.

By having a solid and detailed Forex trading plan any trader is able to know exactly what is reasonable to expect and precisely what to do every step of the way in order to achieve these predetermined goals. Also, by having such detailed plans one eliminates hesitation as well as the great majority of 'surprises' that the market throws at him or her.

Entries are clear, stops are based on rules and reason and an exit strategy is in place. This is done before a trade is executed. All that a trader needs to do is follow the plan knowing in advance that this plan is profitable over the long run. This means that any specific trade might be a loser, but overall the winning trades will compensate for the losing trades and turn a profit.

- A successful trader is disciplined

Now that you know what needs to be done - just do it!

Sounds easy but too many Forex traders encounter this to be a really difficult task. I can assure you that it's not. If you have a good plan that is back-tested and goals that motivate you being disciplined becomes easier.

In time you will learn how to effectively control your emotions and overcome impulsiveness. Although this is somewhat of a challenge, I know that you can do it - anyone can.

- A successful Forex trader follows a sound money management strategy

'There are bold traders and there are old traders but there are no bold old traders'. Forex traders that don't follow money management rules go broke. This should be part of your Forex trading plan but I write it separately just in case. Proper money management rules are crucial, don't neglect this important issue and of course be disciplined!

Here is a thought that many Forex traders don't consider; don't think about the results of one year, think about your accumulated results of ten years. What I mean is simple, if a trader begins a trading account with $1,000 and earns consistent 10% per month, his or her balance after one year will be $3,138. That's excellent results. However after ten years (considering that no withdraws are made), the balance will be a staggering $92,709,068. That's the power of compounding.

MONEY MANAGEMENT IS KEY AND SMALL PROFITS ACCUMULATE.

Protect your capital and get a long term mindset.
I am a firm believer that it is not the system but the attitude of a trader that makes the crucial difference between Forex success and failure. Forex trading psychology plays a significant role in a Forex trader's bottom line; master it and you too will easily become a successful Forex trader.

MASTER YOUR EMOTIONS AND ANXIETY

Ever wonder why about 95% of Forex traders lose money? After all, there are many trading methods that should work, that people swear by, yet two people using the same system can get totally different results. There are also a lot of courses, workshops, mentorships, and so on which should help many more traders make money over and over again.

Yet only a few succeed. Why?

The reason is Forex trading psychology. The reality is that no matter which method you're using, unless you're able to control your emotions, eliminate trading anxiety, and avoid silly emotional trading mistakes.

This is no joke: many losses are caused by irrational trading decisions made by traders who should know better. In fact, psychology explains why two people with the exact same trading education can get totally different trading results.

Controlling your mind and emotions may prove to be the biggest challenge you face as a trader and may help you explode your profits dramatically. Here are some tips:

1. Use stop loss and take profit prices to control your trade. This allows you to place the trade and stop dealing with it. The more you deal with a trade the more it sits in your mind.

2. Just walk away - some traders place Stop Loss and Take Profit prices but then they still look at the trade to see how it's going. Why? What's the point of a Stop Loss if you're going to watch the trade? Are you really planning to interfere with it in mid-course?

3. Use low leverages - The moment you use super-high leverages you do have the potential of bigger profits but also of huge losses. This can certainly drive you crazy with anxiety and lead to bad trading decisions. Until you develop a killer Forex trading psychology, stick to low leverages.

4. Limit your losses to a small part of your account by using tight stop loss prices. Then you will know that in the worse case scenario, you'll be taken out of the trade with a small loss. Nothing to really worry about.

5. Don't use a method you're not sure of. Trust me, if you're going to be trading by tips, or hunches, you're going to be thinking about each trade constantly until it closes. Use a proven, reliable, and structured method and you will be a much calmer trader.

Don't neglect your psychology. Work on your mental fitness. This is a must for long term trading success.

GET THE MINDSET OF THE PRO TRADERS WHO MAKE BIG PROFITS

It's a fact that forex trading can be learned by anyone but most traders fail and the reason they do is they don't understand forex trading psychology. If you do, you can join the elite 5% who make big consistent profits...

So what why is mindset so important?

The simple answer is forex trading is not just about method, it's also about the discipline to trade your method. If you don't have the discipline to trade your system, you simply don't have one.

So why is trading with discipline so hard?

The reason is simply, you will at some point face a string of losses and it happens to even the best traders.

Forget all the rubbish you read, about trading with little or no drawdown, you read from vendors - It's not true. You are going to face periods of losses which may last many weeks and you have to keep going, despite taking losses and your emotions will be telling you to deviate from your plan. Its here, that robust money management and discipline, will carry you through a losing period, until you hit profits again.

Discipline means you have to understand what you are doing and have confidence.

Most traders think they Can follow a so called expert and win, while most advice and forex robots sold online are junk, they cant even follow the few good advisors and forex trading systems because they don't learn from the ground up.

When you operate in the forex market, you operate in an environment that presents these unique challenges:

- The market is all powerful and is always right and only you can be wrong
- Its anarchy and chaos and you will lose for periods of time
- Its an odds based game and you need to learn how to trade them
- There is no rule of law and of course you have to make your own rules to survive
- The work ethic doesn't apply and work rate counts for nothing.
- Being clever also counts for nothing only being right does

In this chaotic and vicious world, your rules and discipline will help you survive and prosper. You can win but remember your method is only part of the equation it's your mindset that is key.

As we said earlier anyone can learn currency trading- but most traders think it's easy or they can follow others. They don't ever bother to learn the basics to get confidence and discipline and they lose.

Forex trading isn't a walk in the park, that's why 95% of traders blow up.
Of course for the serious trader, this presents a great opportunity for big gains.

Forex trading psychology is the key, to putting you in the 5% of winning traders, who pile up the big profits and remember - the market doesn't beat the trader, the trader beats himself. This is generally due to a poor understanding of forex trading psychology.

-How Do I Deal With The Pressure?

You are beginning to like forex trading. You have read every article you can find. You enjoy doing the research, developing your plan and choosing your target currencies. You are comfortable with your forex broker and his trading system. You are gaining valuable experience each day, but for some reason, you are still having difficulty pulling the trigger, perhaps more on sell signals than on buys, but the chatter in your brain is distracting. How do I deal with this kind of pressure?

First of all, let's assume that you have done the basics. You always have a defined and disciplined plan of attack when you approach any market. You do not let yourself get "emotionally married" to any position or pattern that beckons you to stick with it. And, you have learned how to manage your greed and balance it with caution, never backing yourself into a vulnerable position that is difficult to unwind. Now what do you do? The issue now is all about calming the mind, allowing your experiential programming to take over with the good judgment that you have developed, and then reaping the results. There have been many studies in this area, particularly with professional athletes, so why no let them be your guide.

I am a golfer. You never beat golf. You may get better or worse, but the mental aspects of the game are a mirror image of what an individual trader must deal with in order to be successful. Coincidentally, in order to perform, an athlete or trader must be able to shift his focus from distractions and concentrate on the moment at hand. Watch professional golfers on television, particularly when they are putting. One putt per round is all that separates them from the minor leagues, so the pressure is intense to putt well. To deal with this pressure, every Pro has developed his own personal putting routine, i.e., line up the putt, take two practice strokes, look at the cup, and then putt. They practice this routine ad nauseum so that it becomes second nature and requires no thought to invoke it. Then, when the real pressure is on, they do not succumb to any distraction, feeling of doubt or anxious second-guessing.

As a trader, we face similar situations that require quick and nearly automatic responses. Our emotional thoughts do affect our physiology, and therefore, our ability to perform on the spot. Even neutral thoughts can be a distraction unto themselves. The more we can develop a "trading routine", the more dispassionate we can be when we have to execute a Buy or Sell transaction. The more practiced your routine, the more confident you will feel. You will know with certainty what to expect, and performance will become effortless, nearly always exceeding your own high expectations.

So, develop your own personalized practice trading routine. Lay out the logical decision steps and repeat them until they flow effortlessly. Remember that pressure and anxiety can be motivators, but if they are distractions, they must be dealt with accordingly.

WHY MOST TRADERS CAN'T ACQUIRE THIS TRAIT AND LOSE

It's a fact that most traders lose because they don't have mental discipline and the reason for this is quite complex in that to have discipline you have to have certain traits that are not considered good in normal society - but there essential in forex trading.

Forex success is available to those traders who understand the following:

Robust Simple Method + Applied with Discipline = Forex Success

Of course if you don't have the discipline to apply a method with discipline, you really have no method in the first place.

1. Consult an Expert
   The first thing to understand is that discipline comes from confidence in what you are doing. If you don't understand how and why a forex trading system works you will ever have discipline - PERIOD.

To many traders follow gurus or mentors and expect their forex trading system to lead them to success - yet most of the systems sold are junk or the logic is simply not understandable and the traders lacks the discipline to follow it - as soon as it hits a few losses (and all trading systems do) they throw in the towel.

If you take the time and trouble in your forex education to learn all the reasons why a system is likely to work then you can succeed.

Today we are taught that the experts know best but in forex trading this is very often not true.

2. Isolate Yourself
   In life no one likes to be on their own - man is a pack animal and since stone age times we have grouped together for safety. In the forex markets thought follow and join the herd and you will lose your equity so stay isolated.

3. Make Your Own Rules

In life we are taught to obey rules and our lives are structured. In the forex market however we have to make our own rules up and live by them and this is hard for many traders, they simply cannot take responsibility for their actions.

The market is an all powerful force and it moves as when it wishes where it wants to and finally only you can be wrong and it's always right.

You either accept this and construct rules to live by or you fail.

4. Money is Not Important

you have to treat money as if its not. If you don't your emotions will get involved and you will never be able to run profits and cut losses.

Most traders run losses as they don't want to take a small lose and when they get a profit they get so excited they want to grab it before it gets away. Most traders snatch marginal profits whereas if they had held on and had the courage of their conviction they could have made a huge profit.

5. Profiting From Others Failure

Your on your own in trading and its dog eat dog and you make money from others failure it's as simple as that.

Obtaining discipline is simply not easy and as you can see, many traits considered great in normal society need to be re thought. Of course anyone can adapt and trade with discipline in the forex markets it just depends on whether you are prepared to adopt a new mindset.

If you do adopt a new mindset then currency trading success can be yours.

- WHY MOST TRADERS CANNOT ACCEPT BIG GAINS!

It's true, most traders want to make big gains but lack the mindset to do it, let's look at this paradox in more detail.

If you look at any Forex trading chart you will see big trends and they last for long periods of time. It's not
unusual for Forex trends to last for many months or even years so it's pretty obvious that if you lock into and hold these trends you can make a lot of money but most traders have a problem with this and a common scenario will illustrate the point.

When a trader gets in on a trend and it starts to make money, he gets excited and the bigger the profit becomes the more he wants to take it, before it gets away. As open equity dips get bigger, the trader gets nervous and moves his stop up and gets taken out of the market. He then watches, as the trend continues to move the way he thought and pile up thousands or even tens of thousands in profit but he is out of the move and wondering what might have been.

The trader in the above scenario could not take open equity dips and didn't have the courage and conviction to hold the trend. If you want to make the really big profits in Forex trading, you need to accept short term open equity dips and keep your stop back - you need to give the market room to breathe. If you do this, your banked profit will be your reward.

Forex trend following makes money and if you want to do it have the courage and conviction to hold these trends, if you don't, you are restricting your profit making potential.

-ARE YOU READY TO TRADE FOREX

Trading psychology bases its notion on psychology perspectives coupled with the need to prosper. Sometimes that need includes venturing into the forex, or other trading industry. Psychology basis its foundation on the study of human behaviors, patterns, commonality, emotional responses, preferences, etc: Likewise, trading psychology works in the same way.

In the trading industry how you prefer to exchange, buy, sell, or venture is up to you. Some people base their decision on what the current value and earnings are presenting on graphs and charts. The idea of trading however works by staying up with the trends. It has been proven that when ventures stay with the trends they seem to prosper more so than those who jump the rails.

If you are in penny stocks, forex currency exchange, or stock markets it is wise to learn your own patterns. Still, you want to stay with the trends. In addition, you want to mark your behaviors, i.e. you want to avoid taking unwarranted risks. Emotional responses can send you up the river quick; therefore use your mental intellect and common sense when making decisions in the trading industry.

FINDING RESOURCES

Trading psychology news is available online. You will find helpful tips that will guide you in the right direction in the trading industry.

Trading psychology basis its outlook on how informed a person is. If you lack information, skills, etc, likely you are a higher risk than those who learn.

One of the best ways to get started in the trading industry is to read, listen, learn, and try out the free accounts. In forex, trading you can open free accounts, which supply you, live support, help, charts, etc. Watching the daily activities that go on in the trading industry will help you set patterns and become aware of your preferences. Some websites offer free accounts where you use free money to venture in trading. Take advantage of the freebies while you are ahead, especially if you are not clear how the trading industry works:

LOOKING AHEAD

Trading psychology also includes looking ahead. The decision-making process is a personal selection, which should be based on the outlook of the trading industry. You can find references online that will inform you about the history and future outlooks in the trading industry. One of the best tools offered in trading psychology is the notion behind making forecasts based on the well-informed outlook of trading.

CHAPTER 16

DAY TRADING OR LONGER TERM TRADING?

Trends rule in the Forex market. Every trader loves a good, strong trend. As traders, many of us like to make quick profits. Who doesn't? The problem is that by just focusing on making quick profits, we often overlook a much more profitable strategy which is the long-term trend.

First let's discuss the anatomy of a short-term trade. A short term trade can last anywhere from less than a minute to about 20 minutes, if you get really lucky. A 20 minute trade should return huge profits. Those are the uncommon trades and the 1 to 5 minute trade are more common when day trading. As a trader, you must make a split second decision of whether to enter a short term trade.

A savvy trader will set both exit points, profit and stop loss, when entering a short term trade. Most traders, however, set a stop loss, but don't set a goal for their profit leaving the exit at their discretion and, often, to luck. If you do short term trading, set your exit points before entering the trade. You can always adjust them as the trade progresses, but you will be protecting yourself against sudden reversals and changes of market sentiment.

Long-term trading in Forex is often overlooked and even frowned upon by many traders. For one reason or another the belief among most Forex traders is that most money is made scalping the market and that holding positions overnight is not a good strategy. Well... That assumption is wrong. The Forex market is very much like the stock market in that aspect and those that trade the long term charts, whether you use a day or weekly chart, have a better chance of making unbelievable gains.

The reason for it is that, except for exceptional events, currencies make their big gains and losses over longer periods of time and not in a 30 minute time span. If you take a look at the long chart of any currency pair, you will see that, had you traded the long term chart, you would maximize your profits. That is because instead of just making small one day gains on a currency that is trending, you would ride the trend for several days, weeks, and, sometimes, even months. I ask, where do you see the opportunity for bigger profits?

I agree, the long term chart offers a better chance to maximize your profits, but it takes discipline and reconditioning your mindset to stay in a trade for a much longer period of time.

-Combine Both For More Profits

In recent trading times, more and more traders are switching to forex day trading as it promises more immediate profits. However, what most traders miss these days is that it is more important to get consistent profits instead of just immediate gains. But why not have both if you can?

Wise traders now think of combining short term with long term forex trading strategies. Before you reap the benefits of such a combination, it is important to understand both forex trading strategies.

Day trading is a form of short-term trading wherein the same currency you buy are also sold before the market closes for that day. If you do forex day trading, you become an active trader or a day trader. The advent of day trading became even more prominent when electronic trading became more popular. And its
popularity increased when traders realized how much profits such a short term strategy can provide. Forex day trading is undeniably risky, but it also promises such bigger benefits that make the risks worth taking. In fact, day trading has often been compared to gambling due to its fast-paced risk and profit exchange.

On the other hand, long term forex trading strategies are usually implemented by traders for weeks and even months. When long term traders buy, they can decide to hold on to their currency for as long as their long term strategy deems necessary. Long term forex trading strategies are less risky as you have time to plan your moves and to let the market move accordingly then to respond to it.

Due to the more stable nature of long term forex trading strategies, adhering to the concepts of long term trading while doing day trading can give you a more balanced playing field as you trade. By combining both strategies, you get the full blast of benefits both forex trading strategies offer.

Forex day trading offers two main benefits: you get immediate results and you can quickly exit when losses come. So if you win, you get the profits fast. But if you lose, you can make a quick exit so you can minimize the damage done. Aside from these, a fast-paced trading market with immediate results can help a trader become

more adept in the field and can help improve his skills and efficiency in trading.

Long term forex trading strategies, however, also offers a lot of benefits you can also enjoy, such as a more steady run, reduced impact of fluctuations in currency value, benefits from interest rate differentials or IRD, and the ability to correct minor errors in decision-making. All these can contribute to a more consistent and beneficial trading strategy.

WHY YOU SHOULD STAY AWAY FROM DAY-TRADING AND SHORT TERM STOCK TRADING

One of the important principles for maximizing your investment success is to think long-term. Unfortunately, many people spend inordinate amounts of time watching their stock investments and selling after only a short time. Some people sell their stocks after they have owned them for only a few weeks or even a few days. Recent years have seen the increasing popularity of day-trading, in which some so-called investors buy and sell a given stock in the same day.

We believe that investing for the short term, especially the super short-term of a few hours or days, is simply gambling. This is not long-term investing for your future, and there are a number of disadvantages to participating in this short-term trading.

HIGH TRADING COSTS

Many people overlook the commission that they have to pay every time they sell a stock online. Even though online trading has decreased the cost of buying and selling stock, these commissions do add up (especially since some of these individuals perform a huge amount of trades in an effort to make a quick buck).

There is also the bid-ask spread, which is the difference between the price you pay to purchase the stock and the price at which you can sell the stock. Combined with commissions, heavy trading can eat up a significant amount of investment.

MORE TAXES

Selling the stock shortly after purchasing (whether it's a few hours or a few months) opens you up to a higher level of capital gains taxes from your federal and state authorities. If you were to simply hold your stock for the longer-term (more than a year), you would likely qualify for lower capital gains taxes. Remember that what you keep after taxes is all that matters when it comes to calculating your profits.

LOWER RETURNS

Sure, you can get lucky and score big on a particular stock. As a rule, however, investors who buy and hold their stocks for the long term have a greater chance of reaping the rewards in the stock market. If you're constantly entering and exiting stocks, you are spending a lot of time outside of the stock market, and you may simply be missing out on some of the appreciation that more patient investors are experiencing. Whether you like short-term trading because you think you can time the market with some magic formula, or whether you're simply scared every time your stocks come down a little bit, short-term investing could cost you in the long run.

POOR RELATIONSHIPS

This is one that you probably have not considered. However, many people spend way too much time analyzing their stocks. After all, we're talking about short-term investors who simply refuse to buy and hold for the long term. These kinds of day traders and short-term investors have to analyze their stocks constantly so they can decide the best time to exit a particular market.

This can easily become a full-time job, or at least take up a significant amount of your free time at home. Spouses and family members of day traders often report unhappiness because so much of the trader's time is spent closely watching the stock market trends.

DAY TRADING WILL WIPE YOUR TRADING ACCOUNT OUT QUICKLY

One of the biggest puzzles of currency trading for me is that anyone takes day trading seriously as a way to enjoy success. You can't win at it and will lose all your money, the reason is obvious and is the subject of this article. You may be thinking that if no one wins, why are there so many profitable day trading systems for sale?

The answer is:
There all made up in hindsight and simply simulated on paper but have never been traded for real. If you ever see a   track record for a

forex day trading or scalping system which claims extra ordinary profits, then check for the disclaimer:

"CFTC RULE 4.41 - Hypothetical or simulated performance results have certain limitations. Unlike an actual performance record, simulated results do not represent actual trading. Also, since the trades have not been executed, the results may have under-or-over compensated for the impact, if any, of certain market factors, such as lack of liquidity. Simulated trading programs in general are also subject to the fact that they are designed with the benefit of hindsight. No representation is being made that any account will or is likely to achieve profit or losses similar to those shown".

Keep in mind "if it looks to good to be true it probably is" in forex trading if it looks to good simply look for the disclaimer! Your sure to find it!
Of course we can all make money when we know the prices and can trade backwards but you don't have that luxury in forex trading, you have to trade not knowing the closing prices and trade forwards.
The people selling these systems know they wont make money in real time forex trading (otherwise they would trade them themselves) but they know that their buyers will not read the disclaimer to closely, as its hidden away at the bottom of the copy and difficult to see and find!
They then make up some exciting copy to sell it and promise the buyer unlimited riches a regular income etc etc. The novice trader buys and the reality of course doesn't live up to the hype They get a guaranteed profit selling a useless trading system and the trader takes the loss.

Now why doesn't it work - well it's obvious really:

All short term volatility is random in a day or less support and resistance is meaningless and you have no chance of winning because you cant get the odds on your side. It always makes me laugh, when I see systems that claim you can make a living and scalp 100 ticks a week etc - its lies you can't.

You have countless millions or tens of millions of traders, all over the world that make the price, all have different aims, objectives, skills and there all governed by emotions. You simply cannot measure what this vast diverse, volatile, group will do in just a few hours.

Its amazing how sensible people in other walks of life, think they can make money day trading, the logic it is based upon doesn't add up and it is clear to anyone it doesn't work and the facts prove it.

Want the proof? Well here it is:

Ask any forex trader or forex system vendor who claims that forex day trading works, to show you their track record over the long term of gains, audited with account statements. A word of warning here - if you do decide to try and find one, get ready for a long a fruitless search.

Forex day trading is a loser's game avoid it and trade longer term, where you can get the odds on your side and pile up some forex profits longer term.

TRADING THE LONGER TERM TRENDS FOR BIGGER PROFITS

How to Make BIG Profits with Currency Trading Systems FOREX markets turn over trillions of dollars per day and are the world's biggest investment medium.

In recent years, FOREX trading systems using analysis to predict trend changes have increasingly popular as a way of catching profitable trends.

technical become the big Catching the Longer Term Trends for Big Profits

The longer-term trends in FOREX markets mirror the underlying health of the economy. As periods of expansion and contraction take years, so do currency trends and a good FOREX trading system can help you lock into, and profit from, these trends.

When picking a currency to trade, it is important to have good long-term trends and liquidity.

Good major currencies to trade include the US Dollar, Swiss Franc, Euro, Japanese Yen, British Pound, and Canadian Dollar.

FOREX trading systems remove the emotional component from trading, which is the major reason the majority of traders lose.

Removing the Emotion from Trading with Systems

One of the best starting points on the effect that emotions have in trading, are the works of legendary trader W. D Gann, whose works on the subject are essential reading.
Other authors worth reading are: Edwin Lefeurve, Jake Bernstein, Larry Williams, Ken Roberts, Van Tharpe and Jack Shwager whose book "Market Wizards & The New Market Wizards" interviews some of the top traders of all time, including the legendary "turtles".
FOREX Trading Systems for Profit

The developments in computer software, and the growth of the Internet, have seen system trading reach a wider audience than ever before.

Packages such as Tradestation, Supercharts and Omni trader, allow traders to build and back test systems, using technical indicators such as stochastics, Bollinger bands, moving averages, RSI etc., to realistically see how the system would have performed in the markets over time.

Traders who do not have the time, or inclination, to develop their own FOREX Trading systems, can buy a variety of systems off the shelf.

WHAT MAKES A SUCCESSFUL FOREX TRADING SYSTEM?

If you are buying a FOREX trading system from a vendor, there are several things to consider:

1. Do you want to be a day trader, or a longer-term trader? You need to pick a system that suits your personality.
2. Do you want to have any manual input into the system, or do you want it to make all the decisions for you?
3. Do you want to trade just one currency, or a spread? Trading one currency can increase the profit potential, but keep in mind that it can also increase the risk.
4. What is the logic of the system? It is a fact, that if you understand the system and its logic, you will have more confidence in it, than if you buy a black box system where the logic concealed.

5. What is the profit potential and what are the drawdowns? The important point here is that any system will have periods of drawdown or losses, and you need to be able to have the confidence to follow the system through good periods and bad. Generally, the bigger the profit potential, the bigger the drawdowns tend to be.

When you are buying from a vendor, check out their experience, record of accomplishment, customer support etc., and make sure you are comfortable with them.

SWING AND DAY TRADING STRATEGY: USING SWING TRADING TOGETHER WITH DAY TRADING

wing trading (also known as momentum trading) exploits price uptrends or downtrends by entering the market during brief counter-trend pullbacks to ride the trend's momentum. Swing trades can be held for only hours, but more often days and weeks until a trend is played out.

Day trading instead uses minor price fluctuations each day. So you might think that the main difference between day trading and swing trading is the timeframe, right?

After all, swing trading seems like a longer-term form of day trading. They share many of the same principles such as
- Going long or short the market as needed
- Quickly freeing up your capital for the next trade
- Picking more losers than winners to ensure a profitable strategy, and so forth

That's correct except there's one very big difference:

Some of the best day trading opportunities come from counter-trend trading whereas swing trading must always go with the trend.

Does this surprise you? I hope not, because this is how I get my day trades closed out so quickly on most days.

1) I examine the overnight trend in the market
2) Assign specific criteria for when that trend should be exhausted, and then
3) Jump in at turning points for a quick profit

Since most of these pullbacks occur before lunchtime here in Florida, I'm normally done my day trading by that time and therefore free for the rest of the day.

Of course, I look at the bigger, longer-term picture and take the opposite view (trend vs. counter-trend) for when I enter and exit profitable swing trades with the same 75% accuracy. But my swing trades are fewer and farther than my day trades and normally last for several days (sometimes as long as three or four weeks).

Together the two methods synchronize very well to produce a powerful winning trading strategy.

DIFFERENCE BETWEEN SWING TRADING AND DAY TRADING

If you want to be a successful trader, the first thing that you need to decide on is your trading timeframe. This is something you just can't miss or disregard since your trading timeframe can really affect your success. In order for you to decide which timeframe to choose, you have to learn how each works first.

THE DIFFERENCE BETWEEN DAY TRADING AND SWING TRADING

With day trading, traders usually purchase and sell stocks between 9:30 AM to 3:50 AM EST. They make sure that they're out of the market when the clock hits 3:50 AM.
Swing trading on the other hand lasts for 2-5 days. Traders wait for a good price movement before they get in and book a relatively substantial profit.

As you can see, the difference between 2 time frames is the length of the traders' stay in the stock market.

THE RISKS OF EACH TIMEFRAME

The Risks Of Each TimeFrame are always involved when you're trading. With day trading, since traders exit the stock market by 3:50 PM of the same day they entered the market, they don't have to worry about price fluctuations that can happen overnight. Traders can go home, recharge and get ready for another trading day the next day. With swing trading, you'll be holding overnight positions, thus exposing your fund to overnight risks.
Swing traders expose their stocks to overnight risks. There are a lot of things that could happen while the market is closed. Examples of these are release of earnings, mergers, upgrades and so on and so forth. This is the reason why it's really important to place your stop and take profit areas to protect your capital and unrealized gains.

Knowing and placing your stops and take profit areas can save you from losing money while deep in your sleep. Beginner traders are encouraged to start out as a swing trader because day trading is extremely-fast paced. It requires active management and unless you have the experience and skills, you may not be able to keep up.

HOW MUCH TIME DO YOU HAVE?

Because of the nature of day trading, you are required to spend more time in the market and even after the market closes. Day traders are required to intensify their focus on market activities so as not to miss minor shifts in momentum and other elements that can affect their position. So many things happen in just a few minutes that they can't miss. Once the market closes, traders also need to spend a little more time analyzing charts, doing post-trading evaluations and additional research for the next trading day.

With swing trading, you can spend less time managing your trades. You may spend a few hours analyzing market activities, place your trade and visit your stock in a day or so. This is the good thing about swing trading--you don't need to babysit your trade. This makes it really appealing to traders with existing fulltime jobs. They can do their analysis after they get home from work or during the weekend.

BETTER SOURCE OF INCOME

Day trading provides more trading opportunities. This is why it can be a good source of income. Usually, day traders enter into several trades a day and book small profits at a time. On the other hand, swing trading can only provide profits once a week, that's if you entered a profitable trade. If not, then you have to start all over again and wait for another 2-5 days to book your profits.

TRADING OPPORTUNITIES

Day trading offers more trading opportunities as traders take advantage of intraday price movements of infinite number of listed stocks. And as I've said above, they can trade as many stocks as they can handle. On the other hand, swing traders have to look for stocks with longer-term price movements to ensure a profitable trade.

HERE'S WHAT I RECOMMEND:

I recommend beginner traders to start off as a swing trader as day trading could overwhelm them. If you really want to be a day trader, invest in your education, get some experience through demo trading and enhance your skills in the process. Get a mentor or a coach to guide along the way. If you have a fulltime job and may not have enough time to spend in the market, swing trading is also the best route. Day trading requires your full attention and dedication and it requires a lot of preparation.

CHAPTER 17

BECOMING A PROFITABLE TRADER BY KEEPING A JOURNAL OR DAIRY

Do you know what is a forex trading journal? Do you know the importance of maintaining a forex trading journal? A trading journal is a record or a book which keeps track of all of your successful or unsuccessful trades. It is very important for you to keep track of all your trades, whether you win the trade or lose the trade as you can use this information for future trades as a reference. Lets say entered a trade with some reason in specific trading hours, but you lost the trade. The technique might have worked for you earlier but not in this trading hours. With this trade, you come to know that the technique won't work in the specific trading hours. If you don't note it down or keep track of it, in future you may do the same mistake again and you will lose the trade again. A trading journal can be used to refer all the mistakes you did in the past so that you won't do them again. All successful forex traders maintain a forex trading journal.

Trading Forex for a living is different from running any other form of mortar and brick businesses. This is because there is no products to sell, no employee to manage, no customers to attend to and no office place to maintain. Instead, it is only a simple relationship between you and the Forex market.

Once you are inside this Forex trading business for a while, you will start to notice every Forex book that you have read and many other successful Forex traders will tell you about the importance of updating your trades into your trading journal.

Of course, the majority of the Forex traders out there will not even bother to keep track of their profit and loss, talk about writing the journal. But it is really crucial to keep a trading journal to help you to understand not just the actual trades you take, but also why you have taken that trade, how you feel before making the trade, what lessons have you learnt from the trades and how you can avoid the mistakes if you do encounter the same scenario again.

Forex trading is not just about losing or winning pips.At the end of the day, it boils down to your emotional reaction to each win or loss, which will ultimately determine your trading success or failure. By keeping a trading journal, it will not only force you to check on your emotional response to trading, but also show you the logical and illogical reasons that you have for making the trades.

By following the rest of the unsuccessful Forex traders, who do not have the habit of writing a trading journal, they will just simply move on without doing any self analysis or post mortem on their trades. Thus they will not even realise their bad habits and keep on repeating the same old mistakes over and over again.

When trying to profit from currency trading, you need to consider what tools and software are vital to help you towards your trading targets. A forex trading journal should be one of the things that you look to establish as it will have a dramatic impact on your chances of being successful. Often the difference between a novice trader and a professional comes down to accurate record keeping. It adds discipline and structure that are real assets to any trading career.

WHAT IS IT?

A forex trading journal is a notebook, spreadsheet, or other record where you keep details about each trade that you make. These details should include the decision-making or strategy behind the trades. You will also want to note down every detail of the trade, including the date, what currency pair was involved, direction of proposed movement, entry price, planned exit price, the trade size, pips target, pips returned, profit or loss, and the relevant trading session. You can also put in a screen shot of the trade if you want to for future reference.

WHY KEEP THIS?

Maintaining a forex trading journal means that you aren't reliant on your memory to recall the trades that have worked for you and those that went the other way. Trading foreign exchange requires a commitment to on-going learning and you can learn as much from your own experiences as you can from any other source. You will give yourself the best chance to succeed by analyzing the various elements of your good and bad trade decisions. This will allow you to emulate profitable trades and, at the same time, avoid the trades that cost you money.

You will find that a forex trading journal provides benefits in many other ways including the way that it will make you think and analyze your activities. You might be the only one that ever reads it but it still will change the way that you approach future trade decisions. Seeing your trades in black and white can be a sobering experience and adds a dash of reality to what can just seem like paper transactions. You'll immediately find that it will make you think more professionally about what it really takes to make profits over a prolonged period. Having to record something will help to stop you from over-trading or gambling.

LEARN FROM YOUR MISTAKES

When you are trading in the world of foreign currencies, making mistakes is unavoidable. Sooner or later, you will slip up. Do not be afraid of this as it can teach you a valuable lesson. In fact, most of the successful traders found their edge through trial and error. Profits won't come without making some genuine effort to educate yourself as much as possible. Eventually, you will have to learn from your mistakes. And what better way to do that than with a forex trading journal. There is a reason that most successful and respected traders have one and use it constantly. Big financial institutions, banks and companies trading in the market also do the same thing. This really should be the first tool that you think of.

So if you want to maintain your own trading journal what are the important things that you have note down. The following are some of the things that you can note when you start writing your own forex trading journal.

Trading Currency Pair: Note down the currency pair you are trading or you have traded for example EURUSD, GBPUSD etc.

Long or Short: In forex terms Long means buying a currency pair and short means selling a currency pair. Record whether you bought the currency pair or sold the currency pair.

Trade Won or Lost: Record whether you won the trade or lost the trade. If you won the trade note down the reason why you won the trade like any technique you used, any economic news you used to enter the trade etc. Also note down the exit strategy you used for coming out of the trade. If you lost the trade then also you have to note down the reasons for losing the trade.

Trading time: Record the day and time you entered the trade. Also record the time zones you entered like asian time zone, london timings, NY timings etc. This is very important as some trades may work only in specific timings and this information, you can use in future.

Entry Price, Exit Price and No. of Pips: Record the entry price and exit price and also the number of pips you lost or won.

No. of lots you traded: Record the number lots you traded.

Any techniques used: Record any techniques or methods you used for your trading.

Screenshots: Screenshots are very important when you are maintaining a trading journal. As all of us know a picture speaks a thousand words. Even if you note down all the above points and if you don't have a picture, in future, you may not be able to understand your own trade you took. So saving a picture of the trades you are doing is very important.

The above are some of the things that you have to note down if you want to become a successful trader. You may also note down any additional remarks, if you want.

How to maintain a trading journal: Generally forex traders use an excel work sheet or a microsoft word to keep notes of the above things (to maintain trading journal). But when the number of trades are increasing the size of the files also increases.

Moreover when you are saving the screenshots of the trades the file sizes increases more and more. So it causes problems in opening or saving these files. So after a certain point you may have to start a new excel or word file. These problems cause you trouble when you want to sort your trades. For example you want to take a look at all your lost trades or all your winning trades. It is very difficult to sort the trades if you save them in excel or word files.

That is why, forexbees.com is offering you a successful way of maintaining your own trading journal. Once you login to forexbees.com, under navigation block on the left side you will see the link "Create Content". Click on the link and you will see the "Trading Journal" link. If you click on that you will see the trading journal form with the following options you can use when you are creating your own trading journal post. This is completely private and no elase, other than you, can watch your trading journal.

Title: You can enter any title that fits your trade like "EURUSD break out trade - hourly chart - lost" or "GBPUSD MACD convergence divergence trade - daily chart - won" etc. It's better if your title can tell you what type of trade you are doing on the first glance so that it will be easy for you in future to find out the trade you want.

Trade Date: You can select the date on which you did the trade. If you are currently doing the trade you can leave the date as it is.

Vocabularies: Vocabularies are the different categories that you can use to categorize your trades. The following are the different categories available that you can select when creating your trading journal post.

Currency Pair: This category shows the different currency pairs like "EURUSD", "GBPUSD" etc. You need to select the curreny pair you are trading when you are creating you own trading journal post.

Short or Long Trade: If you bought the currency pair you can select the "Long Trade" option or if you sold the currency pair you can select the "Short Trade" option. In forex terminology Long Trade means buying a currency pair. Short Trade means selling a currency pair.

Trade Won or Lost: If you won the trade you can select the option "Trade Won" option or you can select the "Trade Lost" option. Teaser or Summary: Teaser or summary is a small description of your trading journal entry. You can generally copy and paste the first few lines of the body of the trading journal.

Body: You can enter any details about your trade.

Image Picker: This can be used to upload images or screenshots. This shows four tabs. Upload, Current, Browse, Groups. Under "Upload" tab page you can upload images or screenshots of your trades. This contains the image file field using which you have to select the image or screenshot of your forex trade to upload. After that it asks for the thumnail size of the screenshot. I generally use a thumbnail size of 400 px as I like to align the image or screenshot in the middle of the content. "Scale Image" you don't need to use it. "Title" of the image. You can enter any title for the image as this will appear on the top of the image in your trading journal post. "Description" of the image. You can enter any description for the image and this will appear at the bottom of the image.

Once you upload any images you can see them under the "Current Images" tab and also under the "Browse Images" tab. "Current Images" tab shows the images currently updated and only for this post. "Browse Images" tab shows all the images that you have uplodated for all the posts that you have uploaded the pictures. Select any picture. If you have entered the title and description select the "Description" check box. Othewise you won'tsee the title and description that you have entered for that picture. If you want to insert the screenshot left aligned in the body select left option. If you want to insert the screenshot right alighned in the content select right option. If you want to insert the screenshot in the center of the content select the option "none". Click on the body field somewhere. Click on insert button and the image will be inserted in the body field.

File Attachments: If you want to attach the screenshots that you have taken you can use the file attachments and the screenshots will be attached as files to the content and you can download them any time you want.

Once you create a trading journal entry you click on the "Trading Journal" link on the left hand side to see your trading journal entries.

On the trading journal page you can also see the options to sort your trades based on trade dates, currency pairs, trades short or long and trades lost or won.
Calender: Under the calender block you will see a calender which you can use to see the trades on different dates. Click on any date under calender block and you will see the trading journal entries if you entered anything for this date.

Currency Pair: Under the currency pairs block you will see all the currency pairs. If you click on any currency pair you will see any trading journal entries you entered for that pair.

Trades Won or Lost: Under this block you will see two options - Trades won and Trades Lost. If you click on any of the options you will see all the trades you that you won or lost.

Short or Long Trades: Under this block you will see two options - Short Trades and Long Trades. If you click on any of the otpions you will see all the trades you bought or sold.

So this offers a lot of options to you to maintain a very good trading journal to become a successful forex trader. You don't need to maintain your trading journal in excel or word files which take a lot of time to open or save them. You can also upload your trade screenshots or attach them as file attachments.

If you are serious about trading successfully, you need to be keeping a forex trading journal. I remember a long time ago when I first got started trading, I was just doing so so until the day when I decided to start keeping a trade journal.

Your trading will see drastic improvements pretty quickly when you start keeping a journal because keeping a trade journal sends signals to your entire being saying that you are serious with whatever you're doing.

So if you're with me so far and want to start your own trade journal, read on and let me give you a guide as to what should be in your trade journal.

#1 - Record Date and Time of Trade

This will help you refer back to the charts and see when you entered and exited the trade

#2 - Record Currency Pair and Direction

Record which pair you were trading at that time ... be it GBPUSD or EURUSD or whatever. Also record if it is a long or short trade. E.g LONG EURUSD

 #3 - Record Your Trade Entry Price

This is a no brainer ... I personally use Excel for this.

#4 - Record Your Exit Price For Your Trade

The difference between your exit and entry price will determine whether your trade is a profitable or loss trade.

#5 - Record Your Trade Size

In other words, how many lots did you take on that particular trade? If you're trading in mini-lots, record that as well.

#6 - Record Your Nett Pips

Record in numbers ... That way you can see your trading performance at a glance. E.g -22 pips or +34 pips

#7 - Record Your Nett P&L

Make a record of how much you made or lost with that particular trade in terms of dollars and cents. By doing so, you can see which are your biggest losers.

#8 - Record If You Were Trading Countertrend or With The Trend (Optional)

I'm personally very detailed and so I record this sort of details as well.

#9 - Trading Session

If you like you can also record the session you were trading in such as european open or asian close.

#10 - Screenshots (Optional)

Sometimes it will really help when you take screenshots of what you saw at that time you entered the trade.

#11 - Additional Remarks

This column or detail is good for recording how you felt about the trade (before and after it)

You can use your favorite document editors such as excel or word for logging your trades. Ok, this pretty much wraps it all up. Reading all these doesn't help you as much as actually doing it so if you've not been keeping a trading journal, why not do so right now?

Happy trading and happy journaling!

CONCLUSION

Contrary to what every Forex 'expert' out there would have you believe, it's not easy to learn how to trade Forex at all. Trading Forex is one of the most challenging skills you can ever set out to learn, which is especially daunting if you're a beginner just starting out to learn how to trade Forex. If you're finding it hard to learn how to trade Forex successfully right now, you're probably wondering: "Can a beginner make money in Forex trading?" By the end of this article, you'll know what you can do to make money in Forex trading right now.

CAN A BEGINNER MAKE MONEY IN FOREX TRADING?

If you have a look around the many Forex websites, forums, seminars and magazines, it seems like everyone's making millions of dollars trading Forex! The thing is, Forex traders love to talk about their winning trades and make themselves out to be wildly profitable traders, but the reality is that only 5% of Forex traders are consistently making money. Yes, even a beginner can make money in Forex trading, but there's a big difference between making money in Forex and making a full time income, achieving financial freedom, and building wealth through Forex.

What Stops Beginners From Making An Income
So what's stopping beginners from making a consistent, long term income from trading Forex? Well, unlike the professional Forex traders working for the big banks and hedge funds, most beginner traders learning to trade Forex aren't paid a full time salary to immerse themselves in the markets. If you're just starting out in Forex, then you've probably got a full time job that you spend at least 8 hours a day on, and a family and social life outside of that. That means that you have a very real shortage of time to get yourself to the level where you can trade like a pro, and believe me, it takes a lot of time and consistent effort.

It takes years of study, practice and real experience in the markets to learn how to trade Forex successfully, and get to the level where you can consistently make money in Forex trading. Not to mention that you'll be taking on, for all intents and purposes, an unpaid part time job that will chain you to your computer while you are trading. It's something that will alienate you from your social circle, and put considerable strain on your family relationships as well. It's no wonder that most traders wanting to learn how to trade Forex will give up within 3 months, and never make money in Forex trading.

WHAT YOU CAN DO TO MAKE MONEY IN FOREX TRADING NOW

So what can you do to make money in Forex trading right now? The best shortcut I know is to buy a proven Forex trading system to do your trading for you. I'm not going to look you in the eye and tell you that you can just go out there and pick any system and make millions, because that's simply not true. Profitable trading systems are rare, and you need to choose very carefully. That said, if you can find a trading system that works, you can overcome the biggest challenges any trader faces while they learn how to trade Forex. You'll be able to gain valuable Forex market experience, preserve your personal relationships and most importantly make money in Forex trading while you learn how to trade Forex.

When you've built up the capital and income of your Forex systems operation, and have gathered up valuable trading experience, you may decide to try out trading Forex for yourself. Regardless of whether you trade with an automatic Forex system in the short, medium or long term, it's a powerful solution that will enable you to make money in Forex trading even if you're a beginner.

BONUS

10 MOST COMMON MISTAKES MADE BY NOVICE FOREX TRADERS

Do you want to try trading Forex and succeed? Start with learning the most common mistakes beginners make in the foreign exchange market.

1. Intuitive trading decisions. The foreign exchange market is not a casino. However, novice traders view it as such, so they use mainly their intuition to make their decisions. While this may sometimes result in success, but ultimately, the trader ends up failing and losing money.
2. Unreasonable expectations. Some Forex companies promise in their promotions that you'll get rich in no time. Don't believe them. Yes, there are people who end up rich trading Forex, but there are also those who make a fortune by selling houses. In both cases, this does not happen in one day. It can take years to build up the right experience and turn Forex trading into a full-time profitable job.

3. Uncontrolled emotions. The main enemy and biggest mistake trigger of a novice trader is his emotions. When watching the deposit increase or decrease, beginners can lose their minds and take hasty steps to get more money or to stop losing it. This approach is no good. Decision-making should be well-reasoned, rather than emotion-based. In order not to increase tension, place a take-profit and a stop-loss and leave the market alone; don't monitor it day and night.

4. Inability to use a stop-loss and a take-profit. When you place a market order and leave it open, you put the entire trading account at risk. For example, when you open a long position for the EUR/USD pair, you can put a stop-loss so that your Buy order will automatically close if the price falls below a certain level. You can limit the amount of losses for each separate order, especially if you're unable to monitor the market all the time. A take-profit order works the same way: it locks in profits by setting a level at which the position should be closed.

5. Trading against the trend. No wonder they say "Trend is your friend." You can try to catch short-term price movements or price correction. But in reality, you make a larger and more regular profit if you keep track of the long-term price movements and sell or buy in trend direction. Always watch the global price movements over long periods of time and only after that open trades on minor time frames.

6. Intraday short-term trading on minor time frames M1- M15. Beginners may find it difficult to trade on these time frames as they have no experience in time frame synthesis. External factors such as news also matter and can cause problems. In this case, trading can be extremely risky and can lead to large deposit losses. It is recommended to use bigger time intervals

such as H1, H4, D1 and above, where the movements are more predictable and the trader can make wiser decisions.

7. Holding losses for too long. Unlike beginners, and experienced Forex trader can determine when the loss trend is not going to reverse. Instead of hoping for the better, a disciplined trader will take a loss and close the order. Sometimes, life teaches us lessons and we have to learn them and move on.

8. Trading news. When important data are released, prices can move tens or hundreds of pips in either direction within a few minutes or seconds. The movement is so swift that it is physically impossible to trade right. The market is extremely feverish and jumps up and down. Forex brokers widen spreads and reduce liquidity, which entails risks and high loss probability. We recommend beginners to refrain from trading during important economic news release.

9. Too many open positions. If you open too many positions, you are unlikely to respond to all the events properly and quickly. It is hard to focus on each position when you receive too much information.

10. Excessive leverage. Leverage is a double-edged sword because it can improve returns from profitable trades and increase losses on unsuccessful ones. This happens especially in Forex trading, where the trading capital can be depleted if the market entry goes wrong.

Hopefully our advice will help you make smart decisions and trade successfully.

THANKS FOR READING!!!

CPSIA information can be obtained
at www.ICGtesting.com
Printed in the USA
LVHW050042090221
678731LV00029B/1316